SEPARATE MEANS HOLY

Those with Heart Must Stay Apart

by Karen Kellock Ph.D.

A new theory in psychology. According to Koestler, all landmark theories are presented in picture-strip format (right-left integration) to bring on the "aha" experience of the formula (the characteristic of all new paradigms).

FORMULA FOR THEORY:

**ALL SUCCESS ATTRACTION
ALL DISEASE OBSTRUCTION
ALL RECOVERY ELIMINATION**

**The three obstructions are:
people, habit and food.**

**Remove your obstruction and
you snap to your goals,
waiting in the wings.**

SEPARATE MEANS HOLY

What is the Dunning-Kruger? It's the dumb thinking they're smart--most dangerous for sure.   What messed us up? The influence of other people. With trauma we swallow them whole/mimic evil.   Just wanting to pull back, not be included or isolate is taken as an affront, a rejection or insult.   You can tell a social culture by the architecture: front door on street/no fence of protection see.   I mal-adapted to the liberal social culture of low intellect.   A black cloud, I coped with God.   There's no strength in numbers for God's man/the individual is the winner.

DIVINE REVERSALS

THEY'RE IN TROUBLE
YOU'RE THE BOSS NOW
THEY HATED YOUR ANOINTING
PUBLIC HUMILIATION IS COMMON
YOUR FAMILY WENT AGAINST YOU
YOU: RULER OVER MANY NATIONS
LONELY AT TOP AND BOTTOM
KEEP YOUR GUARD UP
BETRAYALS OF FAMILY/SO-CALLED FRIENDS
WHEN YOU HIT ROCK BOTTOM
GOD HAS CHOSEN YOU WITH A GIFT
A WHOLE NEW LEVEL OF ANOINTING
GOD FOUND YOU BROKEN, A RARE GEM

DIVINE REVERSALS

THEY'RE IN TROUBLE

They're in trouble because it says "do my prophet no harm" and "touch not my anointed" too.

You maintained faith in your vision even while it was so hidden. Now it bursts forth as you have risen.

You worked all night when no one saw. While they bragged you remained mute about it all.

One of the worst pains is being betrayed by one's own family. But you were and kept the faith anyway.

You expected people you knew since you were a child to support you but they did the opposite Sue.

All that pain they caused is getting ready to make you millions cuz their wealth is laid up for you kids.

YOU'RE THE BOSS NOW

You're calling the shots now. Your harvest is here and everything you touch is turning to gold, wow.

All those years you suffered are coming back double, even tenfold. You turned rubble into gold.

You were faithful to your people, craft and vision. It was a hard road to greatness but now you're in.

Hard work pays off and you're about to see the harvest. Though underground for years now it surfaces.

Blood ain't thicker than water. Because how could strangers treat you so nice and them the traitors?

DIVINE REVERSALS

How could your own family turn into the strangers? Like you never knew or met them, these traitors?

The only reason they chose not to do right by you is cuz God chose you for the mission, that's the truth.

Your family always saw your light. Though you went thru the struggle it was always evident, aye.

All those years of struggle treated like a nobody was frightening as they pulled you down see.

THEY HATED YOUR ANOINTING

People did what they did due to anointing over your life. Tho' a sinner it helps to know THIS was it, aye.

You knew them all your life but you're a stranger in a strange land anyway: a world filled with strife.

The oil of the anointing destroys yokes, bondages and demonic strongholds: family blockers of old.

Your ex narcissist lover started out fine but then became secretly competitive: more strife.

That was the hell we went thru but look at us now. Look at where God brought you from: bedlam, wow.

Those evil family members and fake friends all look the same. They even colluded together didn't they?

They're all in the same bag as karma came around like a boomerang from what they put you thru man.

PUBLIC HUMILIATION IS COMMON

All that public humiliation, opprobrium and lies they said about you will now come back on em.

DIVINE REVERSALS

Those times they betaryed & mishandled you, made a fool outa you will now come back on em Sue.

They're now humiliated in front of other people cuz you're so high. They can hide but they can't hide, aye.

They're hiding now because of how badly they publicly humiliated you. That's how it works Sue.

They won't ever elevate now that you've gone your separate way. They're stuck but you're great.

While they were publicly humiliating you they really thought they were somebody but now they see.

YOUR FAMILY WENT AGAINST YOU

Your own family chose to go against you. This is an awful lot to chew, I felt that horrible way too.

It's irrelevant you made mistakes. We've all fallen short of the glory of God, we're all sinners/flakes.

Great people in the bible were living in a world full of sin and God still chose them, that's how it's been.

God chose Rahab and she was a prostitute. He chose the apostle Paul and he was a murderer too.

God chose you before the foundation of the world. He knew what you'd do yet chose you anyway girl.

You're in charge now. Everything you touch is turning into gold and will continue to: you're on a roll.

You'll be living your best life now. You'll have the final say-so and all will bow to you as the royal.

You'll have the power and authority to cut anyone off. The butcher, baker or your own sister in law.

DIVINE REVERSALS

You'll be in charge now. You can do whatever you wanna do when you wanna do it, the new royal.

You can move when you wanna move with no one obstructing you again. What a blessed relief man!

You're the boss, the head honcho. God made you ruler over many nations and what you say goes.

YOU: RULER OVER MANY NATIONS

The reason God has made you ruler over nations is so your can draw more souls unto Him, amen!

We had to go thru betrayals to make us stronger. We did things we aren't proud of but then got better.

All the things you endured were just building you and making you wiser. Don't bemoan the teacher.

Believe it or not the betrayals and predations made you more kind and loving despite frustrations.

Now you're in charge and know what to do and what not to do. More than that you have empathy too.

We stay harmless as doves but wise as serpents: made rulers over nations but humble as servants.

They had the opportunity to reign with you but they wouldn't suffer with you so they're gone too.

LONELY AT TOP AND BOTTOM

It was lonely at the bottom but equally so at the top. That's ok tho', we're happiest alone are we not?

You know you are healed when abusers want back into your life but don't let em bac or you'll die.

DIVINE REVERSALS

They shoulda done right by you in the first place but now you're boss it's time to reject them ok.

So-called friends and evil family members always come back so be prepared this time: move on Mack.

KEEP YOUR GUARD UP

Keep your guard up by putting on the armor of God. Pray for a fence of protection around it all.

Forgive and God'll prepare a table before them and turn it all around to your good, it's a promise man.

God showed up on your behalf, making you ruler over many nations. You're back, free and whole again.

Now that you're free and happy again, let's make wiser decisions. You screwed up but it's all forgotten.

Let's be wise now. We don't need narcissists to bring us down again cuz it was no joke dealing with them.

BETRAYALS OF FAMILY/SO-CALLED FRIENDS

Family betrayals and so-called friends treachery is no joke. It was hell on earth being thusly yoked.

Jealousy was as cruel as the grave but now that you're whole and right God'll make them all behave.

From all the stuff we've been thru we should be dead. We hit rock bottom but came back instead.

Once you hit rock bottom you either come back up or that's it. That old life was hellish, wasn't it?

God said "now you hit rock bottom I have your undivided attention" & we made the right decision.

DIVINE REVERSALS

I stopped lethal crutches & life changed for good. Then He gave me a mansion in a loving neighborhood.

WHEN YOU HIT ROCK BOTTOM

When I hit rock bottom God saw my weakness and poured out His spirit upon me, the blessed.

God said "I created you, didn't expect perfection & knew the mistakes you'd make before you made em"

God knew they overlooked me. God knew I was willing to stick it out like a stoic while He prepared me.

I felt vulnerable. I felt I needed people to make it to the next level but they were only filled with the devil.

I was dependent on people but God said "No--I'm gonna separate & teach you" by going solo.

We were abandoned and betrayed since we were children. This was not the only time friends.

GOD HAS CHOSEN YOU WITH A GIFT

Once God has chosen you, put a gift inside and anointed you don't you trust ANYONE Sue.

As hard as you worked for this--your throne--there's someone plottin' & plannin' to take your gold.

We're not lucky. We are blessed and highly favored. Don't you ever let anyone call you lucky sir.

It doesn't matter what you're done if you're gifted, anointed & made in the image of God hon'.

If they've done you wrong and you're fearfully made in the image of God, you should feel sorry for them.

DIVINE REVERSALS

No matter what you're still reigning victoriously. Unscathed from the fiery furnace, deadly.

If you made it back from rock bottom to the mountaintop, you know what I'm talking about.

God never said it was gonna be easy, He said it was gonna be worth it. Who you are now tells it.

Congratulations to you, you're finally in charge now. Don't ever allow controllers in your life pal.

A WHOLE NEW LEVEL OF ANOINTING

You have a whole new level of anointing now. This means your aura is glistening & high: wow!

You're shining so bright, from the inside out. You're pure as a baby again, on top of the world, shout!

With all the hell, betrayals, lies & public humiliations you've been thru, you came out a diamond Sue!

When people left you for dead God found you like a diamond on the beach: in the sand, a rare gem.

When God found you He said "eyes have not seen, ears have not heard the plans I have for you queen".

GOD FOUND YOU BROKEN, A RARE GEM

God found you broken, abandoned & abused and said "look what I've found here", a rare gem too!

Half-way ruined, abandoned, cast off as dross & forsaken: God put you back to royalty, unshaken.

They all didn't believe in you, but God did. And He put you in charge chosen ones while they hid.

DIVINE REVERSALS

While you go back into their presence, just stand there and shine like a trophy. Approved by God see.

God said He approved of you while you were left for dead. That was just preparation to lead instead.

You shoulda given up but instead you gave yourself to God to be used for His glory: to be the head.

But look at you now: looks like you're retiring with the crown. People shoulda never, EVER let you down.

ATTRACTING APPRECIATORS

THE DAMAGED MAKE MISTAKES
THE DEPRESSED DON'T SEE CLEARLY
THEY REALIZE WHAT THEY LOST
DECEIVERS ARE CONFUSED
MARRIAGES PUTS UP A WALL
THE CHOSEN DON'T WANT FRIENDS
STOP SLEEPING WITH THE ENEMY
A MENTAL HEALTH EPIDEMIC IN SOCIETY
THEY SAW YOU AS THE PROBLEM
NEVER GO BACK TO PEOPLE
YOU'RE ANOINTED AND GLOWING
STOP SETTLING FOR LESS
YOU WERE THE BEST THING FOR THEM
CHOSEN FOR NOT BEING VINDICTIVE
THE TREACHERY OF FAMILY MEMBERS
SEE THEM AS SPIRITS NOT PEOPLE
YOU TOLD THEM THE TRUTH BEFORE
THE ENEMY WILL GIVE ADVICE
RELOCATE TO BUMP HANGERS-ON
SURELY GOODNESS WILL FOLLOW YOU NOW
VALUE YOUR REST & RELAXATION
THEY'LL BE IN DEEP REGRET
YOUR OWN FAMILY PULLED YOU DOWN
NEW ONES INTIMIDATE THE OLD ONES

ATTRACTING APPRECIATORS

We have a mental health epidemic in our society. It's seen in the youth and neurotic adults see.

The damaged seem incapable of learning. It's a sad thing but old dogs can't learn/keep renewing.

They can't learn and will always do things the wrong way so keep outa their way and you'll be ok.

THE DAMAGED MAKE MISTAKES

They inevitably make mistakes. From breaking a dish to spilling ink, it suddenly was all I could take.

People make mistakes when they're out of grace. There's a groove we should be in then it's all ok.

There's a divine design to each day & minute. That's when things run smoothly but they're out of it.

Jezebel spirits can't adapt, they just are who they are. Find new friends and free of this disaster.

There's no learning or getting better, they're doomed. And you're lower than them if caught Sue.

When railroaded by these types my vibration was low. It was a bad nightmare reflecting Satan below.

When you're high you see they're guile. They'll get you when you're down and you're in denial.

THE DEPRESSED DON'T SEE CLEARLY

If you're down you don't see it as clearly, it's like a safety mechanism to keep you from painful reality.

ATTRACTING APPRECIATORS

They don't deal with people who are up, only those who are down and can't see reality clearly to stop.

Nobody likes starting all over again but that's how it is after mal-adapting to these ruckus friends.

Getting to know other people, finding a totally different love life. A whole new strata of humanity, aye.

Stop judging on how good they look man. Cuz it's all about their heart and spirit or it's bedlam.

THEY REALIZE WHAT THEY LOST

The only reason that narcissist is coming back is cuz they realize they lost a real one not a hack.

They see you wanted the best for them every day so now let em stay mad they can't have you ok.

How much emotional abuse and heartache can you take chosen one? We all have a limit hon'.

With all the hell they put you thru thank God you didn't have a heart attack but it was bad, a fact.

After a sequence of bad breakups I finally saw I was better off alone. Friends were not my goal.

Being alone means you get your power back. I love every minute of the day: it's fullness not lack.

DECEIVERS ARE CONFUSED

Deceivers are full of confusion. They're toxic, and every time they come back here comes the bedam.

Every time you let em back they drain you then start lashing out. They're not your kind these louse.

ATTRACTING APPRECIATORS

There is power in walking away. Every time you do it God gives you more: it's released obstruction ok?

They'd always come back mad cuz I threw in the towel before. They wanna chew the bone and spar.

MARRIAGES PUTS UP A WALL

Marriage was the best possible solution, putting up a wall. I was saved from hell away from all.

They all put down my marriage partner, of course they did. He saved me from them/the devil's kids.

They put down the institution of marriage, of course they did. They wanted none to save me from this.

You keep em around to save you from loneliness. But that is the greatest if only you could see this.

Why be with somebody who could never love you unconditionally and only wanna suck you dry?

Why be with someone who never wants the best for you or who NEVER pours into you: WHY Sue?

They come back because they see you're happy and winning without em. It's a stab wound hon'..

Once we find we're loved and appreciated we never go back. Predictably that's when they want us bad.

THE CHOSEN DON'T WANT FRIENDS

This is why the chosen don't want friends anymore nor partners nor dealing with families galore.

People have shown their true colors and we're TIRED OF IT. After forty we've had it & are saved from it.

ATTRACTING APPRECIATORS

Every time we're by ourselves we find unspeakable joy God gives us and we don't want anything. else.

Every time we're along we have that peace again. God gives us that power we lost when with friends.

Toxic negative energy drains you. You feel exhausted to the point you stop seeing them as so cruel.

Who has the strength to be alone today? The saints, those chosen by God to be separate ok.

The minute they get back in they seek competition with you. You start going at it then are drained Sue.

STOP SLEEPING WITH THE ENEMY

I cannot believe this. You're sleeping with the enemy? You're making love with your foe today?

The minute you make love with an ex you're committing another illegal soul tie which will regress.

Things won't get any better staying with an ex. There's much better out there but don't go chasin' it.

When alone my mind is fertile: in past, future and cosmic scenarios. When they come it's abysmal.

Because you had more than them you pitied em with your kindness but they just took advantage.

It's the commie spirit of robbing the rich: even tho' you worked hard for it your kindness turns to shit.

A MENTAL HEALTH EPIDEMIC IN SOCIETY

We have a mental health epidemic in our society. It's seen in the youth and neurotic adults see.

ATTRACTING APPRECIATORS

As the chosens we go thru the most betrayal and emotional damage as they all take advantage.

Chosens get treated the worst but they all change later when they wished they had valued us most.

We have a huge calling but always attract the opposite. It's a huge problem and few can understand it.

We need to be alone and work on ourselves until we attract the special ones who are just like us.

You don't have to chase because YOU are the prize. They had you but didn't appreciate you, aye.

THEY SAW YOU AS THE PROBLEM

They acted like you were the problem when you had the aura, anointing and glow of the best one.

They had their chance but of course now they want the goodies that come with you. Never again Sue.

You never give people another chance to mistreat or not value you. That's the way it is, chosens are few.

Strangers treated you as having more value than your own family. This was the frustrating anomaly

Stangers see the best and the greatness in you while those you know were minimizing and cruel.

You can't just hookup with anybody. They must value you not come around to use you for supply.

NEVER GO BACK TO PEOPLE

Never go back to the people who mistreat or not value you. Always giving and being a degraded fool.

ATTRACTING APPRECIATORS

We were the solution but seen as the problem. That why we go solo til God send us those in the know.

You need value. That's why you should be exceedingly grateful you're by yourself: cuz you value you.

Ain't nobody gonna love you like you love yourself. That's where we messed up: seeking help.

The more you put into those people not valuing you, the less valuable you become: imagine that Sue.

YOU'RE ANOINTED AND GLOWING

Here you are anointed and glowing, drained by the users who have no sense of your value darling.

The blessings leave your life cuz you have blessing-blockers around filling you with internal strife.

YOU value you so stay alone until you attract those who do too. That's the long and the short of it Sue.

Those who could not see me were just coming around to get the goodies I so abundantly gave see.

As diamonds in the rough we gotta learn to never take less than what we deserve cuz life is tough.

The past is passed so don't chew a bone over this. Life's in two speeds: you go down then WAY up see.

Bigger and better is your portion so don't take anything else. You've been devalued for too long elf.

STOP SETTLING FOR LESS

Stop settling for anything else than what you deserve. It's astonishing what you put up with, the nerve!

ATTRACTING APPRECIATORS

It feels good to be valued and treasured. Not be used constantly by those who treat you as lesser.

You're getting ready to step into royal status, the best era of your life. Your users can't go there, aye.

You're so good they just naturally fell into the using pattern. They see this now that you're gone.

They played hot potato with your love. They didn't want it then but came back later when deprived of.

When you're gone they felt the impact of your absence cuz you were the realest thing they had once.

YOU WERE THE BEST THING FOR THEM

You were the best thing ever happened to them and they have the nerve saying you were the problem.

You were the solution to ALL their many problems and you mean to tell me you were the PROBLEM?

Because you were the diamond in the rough they threw all kinds of fiery darts at you--it was tough!

We valued them, we saw the best in them while everyone else dogged them out, did we not?

There is great danger and extreme consequences when you touch God's anointed: it's a promise.

The ungodly may see you as average. Think back to high school when you were treated like a savage.

People think they're big & bad--above average--til they run into the Chosen One with true courage.

Your spirit's so powerful they know if they cross you they'll run into God's wrath: it's all subliminal.

ATTRACTING APPRECIATORS

Your essence is so powerful you motivate and inspire people. It's above knowing & transcends evil.

The same people who underestimated and counted you out are put to shame when they see you again.

CHOSEN FOR NOT BEING VINDICTIVE

One reason you're chosen is God knows you're gonna show him the right way: not seeking revenge ok.

If you hold your peace and let God fight your battles, victory shall be yours. That's how it is brothers.

People know exactly what they did to you. Karma is whipping their behind, that's how it is Sue.

God will bring em back into your life so they see: God'll make em your footstool, then you're free.

Those family members who minimized you: well, they gotta eat crow too. This thing is biblical Sue.

They can see you're elevated, that God's favor is over your life. Everything they stole came back, aye.

The wealth of the wicked is laid up for the righteous and those who did you wrong shall see it sis.

When God said He'd lay out a table before your enemies He meant just that IF you forgive their treachery.

THE TREACHERY OF FAMILY MEMBERS

The treachery of family members is the hardest to forgive. decades are wasted we coulda lived.

God brought me out of a raggedy old ghost town and put me in place befitting a royal priesthood, wow.

ATTRACTING APPRECIATORS

How you respond to being mistreated and used determines how much God blesses you too.

Going along with being exploited all to avoid loneliness damps your blessings & creates forebodings.

Stop trying to take people with you to your next level. They've just been using you so they can't go.

Don't ruin your new year by bringing back old relationships when you've grown way beyond it.

SEE THEM AS SPIRITS NOT PEOPLE

Stop seeing people as people but rather as spirits. As you sharing a bed with Satan? Think. about it.

Stop chasing after relationships & people. You. should be chasing after your assignment not evil.

We do not chase, we attract. When you stop chasing it all comes to you for you're the chosen: fact.

For right now you're just better off alone. Number one, no distractions. Two: there's no on using you.

When alone there's no one causing confusion and chaos and that allows growth and continued progress.

Conserve your energy for the next level. Because a relationships takes a LOT of energy for real.

When God isolated us He gave us escape from generational curses so learn to love aloneness.

God put you in a high position due to your heart. You fell but got back up again with a fresh start.

Don't you share your blessings with exes who did you wrong then. Go forward with all new friends.

ATTRACTING APPRECIATORS

Now when we fall and make a mistake our spirit is suddenly convicted and we feel so bad ok.

They hated Jesus for preaching facts because they were living a lie: deep in sin, punishment and lack.

When you have the holy spirit inside you can read people like an ex-ray machine: thru & thru.

YOU TOLD THEM THE TRUTH BEFORE

You told em the truth before & they didn't get it. So why go tell em again? Stop wasting your energy man.

The more prayer the more power. Your discernment grows so you can see a lying spirit better.

When God isolated you went way past them so aren't you glad He made you alone w/out friends?

You're coming up with new ideas, you're starting your own business all due to the dreaded "loneliness".

You know when they're jealous, you know when they're throwin' crap on your success: that's your guests.

The manipulative scumbags living in a world full of sin will even advise you-- but you can see through.

Your ex friends are doing the devil's work but you've got discernment and won't give in to the jerks.

THE ENEMY WILL GIVE ADVICE

Your enemy will even advise you on what you should and shouldn't do, which you instantly see thru.

God gave you blessings cuza what YOU'VE done so don't you go giving em away to those bums.

ATTRACTING APPRECIATORS

They want what you have but hate what you say cuz it convicts them ok. just as Jesus brought hate.

You just enjoy your blessings and continue to grow while they stay back stuck in their swill so low.

They don't have much cuz they've done too much so when they hit you up tell em NO/out to lunch.

RELOCATE TO BUMP HANGERS-ON

You'll have to relocate to rid all these hangers-on who keep asking and begging like little children.

But you just continue your good works and wonderful routines, God'll keep blessin' you see.

They'll never be anything cuz they don't wanna listen to reason nor do the work of God, their salvation.

They eat or. drink all day with complete irregularity while you fast and pray-- who's God gonna bless today?

You work all day on what God's assigned while they manipulate and plan how to steal from the man.

Once you get into the daily groove of prayerful work and routine you can relax the rest: it's so serene!

He prepared a table before me in the presence of my enemies so of course they wanted to use me.

SURELY GOODNESS WILL FOLLOW YOU NOW

He anointed my head with oil and my cup ranneth over so of course it attracted frenemies/ex lovers.

Surely goodness and mercy shall follow my all the days of my life lest I let em back in to create strife.

ATTRACTING APPRECIATORS

If free of wicked I shall dwell in the house of the Lord forever. In freedom these were my words declared.

Why is power in the pen? Cuz people don't know what to think, why they're here or why things happen.

VALUE YOUR REST & RELAXATION

You can listen to music & watch movies all you want as long as you do His work assigned, when you want

I love music, movies and walks in the breeze. If I didn't have R & R I'd go crazy so I do as I please.

Avoid compulsive work activity and tunnel vision. Work when inspired and spend your time buildin'.

Good R & R is what you need to inspire thee so the work remains rich, relevant and keeps you happy.

I don't need travel I just need a computer to keep me inspired as long as what I watch is high tiered.

You know what you've been thru and what you've overcome. You deserve it all now so avoid the bums.

Your evil family members and so-called friends shoulda done right by you for you've finally healed Sue.

THEY'LL BE IN DEEP REGRET

While you've been born again they're in deep regret. That's how it works when things reverse pet.

While you call the shots now never forget how they mistreated you and don't ever go back.

Like the story of Joseph and his own brothers, they left you for dead and even called you a monster.

ATTRACTING APPRECIATORS

Joseph's own family sold him out. Like a black sheep stripped of his inheritance, it hurts s lot.

They didn't know God was stirring up that gift while you were in the pit. Molding & shaping, all of it.

You weren't just a diamond in the rough but the bottom of the pit as they treated you like shit.

YOUR OWN FAMILY PULLED YOU DOWN

Your own flesh and blood family kept pulling you down, wrecking your good reputation all over town.

You told them of your dreams & goals and they shot them down. God had to separate you all around.

God literally called you to lead but instead you were trying to fit IN with people despite their evil.

People didn't believe in/pulled you down but since God was for you, no one could be against you.

While you're going thru the pit-to-palace transition God will bring you before appreciators of you son.

Now God will finally put you with people who believe in you and who will actually fight for you!

Your new friends will intimidate your old ones because you're at a whole new level now, and what fun.

NEW ONES INTIMIDATE THE OLD ONES

Your new family that God gives you will intimidate the old one who rejected you: what a new view!

You are above and beyond everything now. Your new partner will intimidate your ex or old pals.

ATTRACTING APPRECIATORS

Families will now be blessed through you as you have the anointing of your life and so wise too.

When God has His hand over your life there's nothing anyone can do anymore to destroy you, aye.

Joseph was at the bottom of the pit though he could interpret dreams and had other incredible gifts.

JUST BE ALONE

NO WINNING WITH A NARCISSIST
PREPARE FOR YOUR COMEBACK
SET A BOUNDARY, PREPARE FOR DISCARD
YOU ARE THE RISING STAR
GOD GIVES BACK DOUBLE/TENFOLD
BORN TO STEP INTO CALLING
THEY SAW YOU AS A NOBODY
YOU CAME OUT AS PURE GOLD
GOD IS GETTING READY TO MOVE
THEY'LL DEPRIVE YOUR FINANCES
THEY GET ANGRY CALLING EM OUT
THE WEALTH OF THE WICKED
HOW KINDNESS IS RUINING YOU
THEY SHOW NO SYMPATHY
THEY BEGIN GREAT
THE HOLY ARE SEPARATE
IN THE PIT TORN TO PIECES

JUST BE ALONE

NO WINNING WITH A NARCISSIST

There's no winning with a narcissist so the only way to win is to go no-contact and be yourself again.

The narcissist won't change because the amount of work it takes and the demons in them ok.

Change takes deep inner work that most narcissist will never go thru ever, they can't be told a thing sir.

It's possible to recover but not probable so if you're stuck with a narcissist get out on the double.

Getting yourself back means coming to success. It's by the pure grace of God, unobstructed by that mess.

After all the gossip and rumors about you, you shine bright like a diamond ready to build too.

Other people left and forsook you but look at you now, a bright light for all to learn from and love, wow.

PREPARE FOR YOUR COMEBACK

Your comeback will be much bigger than your setback. It's gonna be incredible and an historical fact.

You've been challenged for so many years. People've been in competition and it's brought you to tears.

You are a STAR and that's why people suddenly turn on you and start talking about you: you're marked.

When it comes to what you do you're the star in the sky, the world's greatest cuz you were born to do this.

JUST BE ALONE

They will hurt you then question why you're not there for them. It makes no sense in pure contradiction.

When you set boundaries & the narc acts like an entitled kid who does it anyway, its a dead giveaway.

Narcissists hate the word "no" and if you put a boundary on em it's like they've been hit, brought low.

SET A BOUNDARY, PREPARE FOR DISCARD

You set a boundary & they'll discard and go to someone else working their magic as black elves.

You hit rock bottom but came up again an entirely new person and will never drop again, amen.

There are some who relationships bring down to rock bottom. The undertow is severe I fathom.

You know you were born to be a star when you make it back from rock bottom with no help at all.

When everyone ganged up on you and you still won, you know you're a star so just give it time hon'.

All the evil things that came from you was the devil, it wasn't you. Put it al lin a bag and forget it Sue.

It wasn't you, it wasn't you. Put it all in a bag and cast it to the bottom of the ocean then don't go fishin'.

They meet you today and you're a perfect lady. No one would ever dream those things were you see.

YOU ARE THE RISING STAR

You are the rising star. Coming up from the depths of rock bottom everyone will know who you are.

You are the well-known unknown. A universal archetype instantly recognizable and glowin'.

JUST BE ALONE

As a rising star God will make your name famous, after going through all that and up again unscathed.

What drug you down was people and your addictive devices to adapt to them and their evil.

I spent my life trying to get away from them. I wanted only isolation and now I finally have it, amen.

The world is too much with me. It is only cacophony: noise, confusion, manipulation and blasphemy.

Did we have to go thru all that and sink so low? Well yes, I think so. The depths then fame, to show.

GOD GIVES BACK DOUBLE/TENFOLD

Everything I lost God gave back to me double. I am entirely blessed after going thru that hell.

In order for us to be FIRST right now, we had to be LAST first--does this seem strange somehow?

We had to take the BACK seat as hated inferiors in order to be placed in the FRONT seat as loved superiors.

They told jokes about you and laughed at you. You felt so alone but now you're on top, well-shown.

You were born to be separate, a star. But first you had to feel calumny & opprobrium of a deposed czar.

You had to go way down in order to go way up. There was no other way to fame and what a trip.

You lost all your friends, most who you'll never see again. It's a sad trip only for champions, amen.

Most couldn't take half of what you've been through. You went thru the ringer but came out new.

You've been tried & tested so now God's ready to show you, uncontested. What a trip awaits God's best.

JUST BE ALONE

This is why relationships and marriage didn't work out sir. Because you were born to be a star!

No one could understand nor get along with you, for how could they? It's like a horse and a donkey.

You were born to do God's will, so how could you get along with those groupies who are useless still?

BORN TO STEP INTO CALLING

You were born to step into your calling when the hell you went thru was finished. You're now famous sis.

God had big plans in store. for you. But first you had to find out about humans flawed thru and thru.

Only God's plans for you will prevail, not your plans which will never never work and always fail.

God hates your enemies and took em all out early. Look at em now, can you even find em? No way.

Your ways would never work cuz you didn't put em in God's hands. You weren't trusting in Him man.

We came from the bottom to the mountaintop. That's the trip of royalty: until the end we'll never stop.

God has made you the center of attention and now's your time to shine and give it all you got hon'.

THEY SAW YOU AS A NOBODY

All those years people saw you as a nobody but with God you're gonna be the next big thing see.

Because God wants to use you for His glory, it's far bigger than we think it is, outa this world see!

JUST BE ALONE

For the people who didn't believe in you, this had to happen so God could flush em out, the forsaken.

It had to happen so the people who betrayed and sold you out could be visibly shaken and cast out.

You'll be so elated you'll say "thank you Lord for allowing this to happen: my struggles and all", amen!

"Thank you Lord for allowing the hardship cuz look at how I came out: wonderfully made and perfect!

YOU CAME OUT AS PURE GOLD

You came out as pure gold, a diamond in the rough. Imagine that after pulled down to hell's stuff.

The worse it was, just imagine how you're gonna look when you come out and away from the scuzz.

When I stepped into my life's purpose I cut off family and friends for a whole year and won sis.

You gotta leave the past behind you. Family, friends and those memories of hell & being utterly screwed.

You gotta give up everybody for what God has for you. If you wanna be held back keep hanging out Sue.

Some of us wasted all our thirties and forties hanging out. It's a social generation and a waste, ouch.

GOD IS GETTING READY TO MOVE

God is getting ready to move on your situation for future. But you're still hanging out with lechers?

Regardless of your age, as long as you have breath in your body God said you could do ALL THINGS.

JUST BE ALONE

Many who are stars right now had humble beginnings. Tho' big now it took em decades of suffering.

Stop listening to people who aren't getting you where you need to be. The social world is pure cacophony.

People plot and plan behind the scenes. They rub your head while trying to get your money see.

"Oh yah that girl's real nice and she got money". Then they plan how they gonna get some honey.

THEY'LL DEPRIVE YOUR FINANCES

They'll deprive you of finances then try to get your body too. Humans are dirty rats and the good are few.

You gotta be ten steps ahead in the game with these manipulative scumbags all around you ok.

You must keep your head on level & constantly be in your prayer closet. Don't let em get close, the sick.

The more you pray the more God reveals who people really are cuz the holy spirit knew em before.

Your isolation will make you very wealthy. Stay focused because God is preparing you for prosperity.

Being alone doesn't mean lonely. For me it means wide worlds opening up to splendor and prosperity.

THEY GET ANGRY CALLING EM OUT

When you call them out on their B.S. they get mad at you. Get the police or anything you have to do.

People left you but God isolated you. He removed those who can't go where you're gettin' ready to go to.

JUST BE ALONE

Before your reaction they were little angels but now demons are coming out: how predictable.

They do things deliberately so you get into it, so they won't pay you back: that's the truth Mack.

Is loyalty too much to ask for? At this point of your life, it is. You get sick and they won't be there sis.

The righteous are never forsaken nor their seed begging for bread. Your foes are facing karma instead.

THE WEALTH OF THE WICKED

The wealth of the wicked is stroed up to give to you, the righteous. That's their karma and yours sis.

"Lord, they meant it for evil but thanks for turning it around to my good". That's how it works or should

They stole from you but God will prepare a table for you in their presence, that is the holy word's promise.

You don't have to worry about these people paying you for what God has is only yours and far more too.

Keep your grass low to see all the snakes. After all you've been thru you've had all you can take.

I'd rather be alone then around a buncha manipulators. Never be afraid to be by yourself in God's favor.

HOW KINDNESS IS RUINING YOU

You must wake up and see how your kindness ruined you. It's wrecked the lives of more than a few.

Stop trying to play hostess with the mostess. Your guests are just users and you're busy miss.

JUST BE ALONE

The Lord said to keep our peace but sometimes you gotta SPELL IT OUT for them, again & again.

Your kindness has ruined you your whole life. It's time to put your friggin' foot down or simply die.

If you continue to let people see your kindness as weakness you will never be the strongest.

I secretly hated my guests and the time wasted but being the weakest I went along with it sis.

They just see your home as a repository of all nice things and happy times: cut em off or die!

Once God exposed them you still want them back? Shame on you, where's your self-worth at?

THEY SHOW NO SYMPATHY

They show no sympathy for you while you're constantly breaking your back for them: see the system.

They hate the truth, preferring to dumb you down. It's very frustrating if you're a smart/good person.

They're living down in an evil shadow ready to mess you up. Don't be gaslit, there's little you can do to help.

There's nothing you can be ready for, messes just happen. There's no predicting the forsaken.

It is so dangerous to be around these haunted houses. Before you know it there's trouble/messes.

She let me dog outa the fence. She brought another louse who caused offense. She was just dense.

Could it be it's just this generation? People were mannered in the fifties but I don't know son.

JUST BE ALONE

All I know is I don't dare let em in. They'll ruin your life and house for it's an adulterous generation.

This is what happens when you spare the rod and don't teach the old ways. Bedlam, ruin and cacophony.

It's good to be aware but it's not enough. You must stay outa range of these dimwits and troubled nuts.

THEY BEGIN GREAT

They begin great, very impressive. But then there's a slip and you see the real person: don't miss it.

Getting involved with a nutcase can take you years to get back. Don't minimize the dangers: fact.

These people are very "powerful" but in a low vibrational state. They're very dangerous in every case.

You can't help, it's a spirit in them. All you can do is stay away and pray for them/learn your lesson.

They hate the truth, their truth is the truth but it's not so you've had it hanging out with the uncouth.

They're like kids--they want things the way they want it to be but it's not the right way, the only way.

They're not taught right, not taught properly or trained. They're like little puppies going every which way.

THE HOLY ARE SEPARATE

The holy are separate, then they can progress with ease. Don't get stuck staying with the sleaze.

Such is the adulterous generation, a buncha kids in adult bodies. We're led by evil children see.

JUST BE ALONE

They are damaged human beings always doing things the wrong way & taking you down with em ok.

I was advised by an old woman to take em in, maybe to help them. They trashed the place/created bedlam.

You're the one thinking right but they call it wrong. You're a laughing stock to the evil throng.

IN THE PIT TORN TO PIECES

Being in the pit torn to pieces will be the last mistake you ever make in this life after releasing it.

There have been many adulterous generations as described in the bible: monsters and great evil.

I met tem again in their fifties, they'd spawned many children outa wedlock. They were zombies/drugged.

Not doing things the right away but only the way they want it to be is the evil way: dark children ok.

They carry dark energy, aye. They're very off, you can't tell em anything so save yourself and don't try.

They'll hear what you're saying and may even agree but they're not gonna change: try it, you'll see.

Spare the rod, spoil the child: maybe for the rest of their days so be separate and achieve your own style.

SEPARATE MEANS HOLY

Those with Heart Must Stay Apart

CUT SOUL TIES & TIME WASTERS
STRANGE WORLD: CAN'T GET WELL
THEY HATE WHAT THEY CAN'T FIGURE
THE SUCKING SPIRIT
STRANGERS
BORREGO BLUES
ANTI-WOMAN HATE STRAIN
LIBERAL TYRANNY AND AL-ANON
WE DON'T ALL MIX YOU TWIT
MORE TROUBLE THAN THEY'RE WORTH
HIX POLITIX UPDATES
PEOPLE WASTE YOUR TIME
CHOSEN AS A VESSEL
WANTING PRIVACY IS AN AFFRONT
DUNNING-KRUGER: DUMB THINKING THEY'RE SMART
SOCIAL IS NOT GODLY
MUST KNOW THY HISTORY
MY HOME IS NOT YOUR PIT STOP
BAD ASSOCIATIONS AND YOU
SCAPEGOAT SYNDROMES
"LOVE TRUMPS HATE" MEANS F-YOU
HE'S KILLING UNELECTED SECRET GOVERNMENT
WOMEN'S MARCH OF SORE LOSERS
FEMINISTS ARE DANGEROUS
FEMINISM AND OTHER LIBERAL SCAMS
MALE BASHING AND WHITE TRASHING
WOMEN ENCOURAGED TO DIVORCE
LIBERALISM IS A MENTAL DISORDER
CURSE: ILLEGAL ALIENS COME FIRST

SEPARATE MEANS HOLY

Those with Heart Must Stay Apart

VIOLENCE IS INTEGRAL TO LEFTIST VIEW
LEFT HAS NO OBJECTION TO CHAOS
EDUCATION THE GREATEST WEAPON
IDIOCRACIES GET WORSE THEN DIE
TRUMPSTERS NEED PROTECTION
POP CULTURE REFLECTIONS
SOCIAL HYPNOTISM OF HERDS/TRIBES
CHILDISH DEMOCRATS LOSING LUSTER
TWO AMERICAS: CRAZY COASTS VS. HAPPY FARMERS
HE FALLS IN MUD AND COMES BACK UP
THE LEFT HATES ANOMALIES
TWO-FACED FOX IS CACOPHONOUS
GENDER OFFENDERS
BLIND CULTURAL RELATIVISM
LIBS FELT SUPERIOR FOR FOUR DECADES
MASS MENTAL ILLNESS IN LIBERAL CULTURES
I HAVE A RIGHT TO OFFEND YOU
A DARK WORLD WITH NO FREE SPEECH
MEDIA: THE FAKE BECOME RANK
CONSEQUENCELESS HEDONISM
STRENGTH VS. BASKETCASE VICTIMS
CRIMINALIZATION OF POLITICAL DIFFERENCES
WHERE ARE THE WHITE SUPREMACISTS?
IT'S A BABY NOT A POLYP
LOW FAT AND LUSTROUS SKIN
LIGHTER, PURER, WISER
LIKE PSALMS SAYS THEY HATED YOU
THE OTHERS ARE CALLOUS
ALL FLUFF OR PERFORMANCE?

SEPARATE MEANS HOLY

Those with Heart Must Stay Apart

Once you see him there is no going back. It's over, he's been depedestalized and that is that.

And oh what a horrible day that is. When you and everyone sees the bloat of fakers.

Once having seen the cad for what he is, only if drunk or mentally insane would you be with him.

Whether in normal or insane phases, we need to understand SOCIAL not abnormal psych.

When you tally up pros & cons, ups & downs you see you gained nothing from these clowns.

Alone you're a dynamo but surrounded by evil helpers you're dragged down, boring and slow.

Living in a small liberal town was like a constant black cloud of reactions and status tension.

Who said what to whom, proving them wrong: My God was my champion fighting the throng.

CUT SOUL TIES & TIME WASTERS

They're more trouble than they're worth. You'll be so much happier when back to you, the First.

Don't fret when the wicked flourish like an olive tree cuz tomorrow they'll be mowed down see.

Don't colab unless they do half the work. Social outreach may suffice if you hate that part.

SEPARATE MEANS HOLY

Get this soul tie outa your mind, always talking to him. Return to self and talk to God your friend.

You'll be so much happier after separation because now you don't sense that constant rejection.

Cut him completely loose. End that cycle and start a new one as nature abundantly substitutes.

Since most modern audiences have a liberal bias it's not that easy to be a conservative comic.

I laid a boundary and you busted it. Now you're mad there are consequences, what a twit.

There's nothing so ugly as youth without knowledge asserting their cramdowns from college.

This isn't the fifties. There's a strain of women-hate that came out against me/I want privacy.

Genius is so innately wired to his inner world the outer is constant upset [needs management].

Genius throughout history worked all night when the herd was asleep, it makes total sense see.

The idea of an INNER LIFE--the true religious experience--is lost to the social nutcases.

You don't get anything FROM a narcissist, they just take what they want and then claim credit.

A narcissist is such a chameleon he can adapt to any situation but you can't count on him.

STRANGE WORLD: CAN'T GET WELL

SEPARATE MEANS HOLY

No one gets well in an Eating Disorder group since the tyrants ban any talk of how to improve.

You're a young man trying to make sense of a crazy world so I've given you a psych tool.

The tool is this: they're all crazy. The road to hell is wide because they're hypnotized socially.

Even conservatives and the religious can have a liberal bias cuz it's been so drummed into us.

Men are interested in sports or whatever but women are interested in relationships forever.

Slavery was all over the world. Indians and blacks had em & there were white slaves from Ireland.

You're so exposed in a small town as word gets around. You're living right but they're dumbed down.

The RELIEF from losing soul tie like explosion of rockets after energy held down by lunatics.

To be in a cozy country neighborhood where all mind their own business is a heavenly oasis.

All the women were crazy idiots when it came to gossip. That's how they ruled: getting ALL of it.

Then they're mean bitches the minute they feel an edge over you cus Mrs. Jones said it was true.

It was total torture dealing with their obvious misjudgments but I just had to put up with it.

But you don't understand. I'm a genius and art and science discoverer going down in history ma'am.

THEY HATE WHAT THEY CAN'T FIGURE

SEPARATE MEANS HOLY

If they can't figure you out they're gonna have a problem with it that's the long and short of it.

Yours is built on a strong foundation from years of gradual work but there's isn't save twerks.

There fake destiny's built on bloviation and bloat--salesmanship--and we're even told that's it.

Well it's not. Success is bricks in a building until that last one then you're done. Takes time hon'.

First you separate from time wasters and no more drop-ins cuz the bored ALWAYS wanna come over.

You're an exciting person to be around so the bored and lonely SUCK you dry til it's you they own.

THE SUCKING SPIRIT

It's the Sucking Spirit that wants everything not nailed down. They wanna conquer you, man or woman.

This isn't the fifties [all about geniality cuz they'd all suffered so greatly] it's now social treachery.

I recall adapting to lunatic landlords and bosses but that was all preparatory to being the mostess.

I learned more than library of books as your scapegoat when you knew nothing about me you kooks.

Without the verbal skills to stand up against you when ten all that anger went into depression.

Worse yet in my searing pain and shock I bought a dam lie and the ramifications lasted for life.

Transcend all group, tribe, family & cultural views of humans: this is God which is universal man.

SEPARATE MEANS HOLY

It doesn't mean you don't hold on to your own, it just means you get clarity within you alone.

I know it still stinks right now but God cleanses reality and memory. It's paradise, you'll see.

STRANGERS

It's hard enough learning the ropes [of social dopes] in your own culture but now we got strangers.

Whether it's apartments or Bed & Breakfasts in country districts it's still STRANGERS amongst us.

Obama/Biden will invade neighborhoods with apartments [strangers] and we don't want it.

We had perfect privacy in our country neighborhood til their dam B & Bs changed it all God!

Anyone clear would be leery of a car accident but they drive like bats outa hell, minds absent.

In an instant life is changed forever: maimed or dead, whatever. I stay home, you go out sir.

Some of these strangers don't like our dogs and there are other problems besides dear God.

I moved to a country neighborhood for a reason so it's a real incursion, a form of neighbor treason.

They invade our land through IRENT as neighborhoods fall into commercial zones and investments.

My neighbor's dog was shot. Strangers from far away lands don't love man's best friend you nut.

Long term relationships trusted but with strangers you're always orienting to novelty at best.

SEPARATE MEANS HOLY

I moved to beauty and for the privacy so your B & B's will force me to move again unfortunately.

BORREGO BLUES

Borrego it was a great learning experience but I'm so glad my Ph.D. in the Streets is complete.

It's painful to be unjustly accused of horrible things, to be seen in that light when you're a king.

Beethoven was hated in a small town and the kids abused him the worst as genius is cursed.

After lifelong persecution Soren Kierkegaard's tomb reads "now just with Jesus will I speak".

Move to beautiful resort town with palm trees and the human element instantly blocks the queen.

The jealous females instantly sized me up and out came the swords and their relentless gossip.

The men in town acted like they owned me. It was surrealistic, was this the middle east?

In a social era they chum up quickly so the stand-alone genius is targeted as hateful/unfriendly.

Chummy, gluey, clammy, imposing, gossippy, catty and divisive vs. the walled-in lofty separatist.

I liked you at first but now you bring evil gossip against me and my happy life is filled with bees.

ANTI-WOMAN HATE STRAIN

Especially a single woman is easy game for the mentally lame who joyfully put her thru hell ok.

SEPARATE MEANS HOLY

Grifters dropping in and taking over the home with porous boundaries by a dumb woman.

A genius becomes so isolated he thinks he needs to trust someone so settles for a bad fink.

The solution: find someone who loves you/you love and then it's you TWO against the crazy world.

Mirroring is not the same as empathy. He'll copy your preferences like he agrees/is trustworthy.

Narcissists know how to work a crowd. You're just one among many being done simultaneously.

To love men you must distinguish the psychopaths from the others who are kind, helpful, generous.

To love women you must distinguish Jezebels from the others who are sweet ladies and girls.

You can spruce them up but they're still a jewel in a pig's snout, losers and con artists, dubs.

Even if offense occurred only yesterday it's wise to think "oh well, we were younger then ok?"

Don't go low: If they ask a personal question [none of their business] you don't say YES or NO.

Boundaries are linked to consequences: If you are mean or callous I will remove myself.

It's about honor, aye: America saw Afghanistan as the biggest example of dishonor in our lifetime.

LIBERAL TYRANNY AND AL-ANON

I grew terrified of Cindy. It was her wagging tongue going to Al Anon gossiping against me.

SEPARATE MEANS HOLY

Of course the recovering alcoholic husband hates Al-Anon, that's her forum proving him wrong.

She talks against him at Al-Anon then they all know about his antics to destroy a woman.

She didn't have the verbal acuity to debate with me so went to Al-Anon and they ALL agreed.

Gossip is wrong but somehow it's all ok if it takes place in Al-Anon when they laugh at her man.

Seething with resentment she can't wait to get to Al-Anon to unload it for their amusement.

I'd never live in a small town again after that. It's as bad as Al-Anon in their gossipping called chat.

We're dealing with violent, dumbed down, brainwashed people so be bold but sweet & humble.

They got their way for years from pugnacious threats that worked [we cowered and shirked].

Young men can be all instinct without constraint or moral regulation and I'd say avoid em.

As she's always on slow boil under the surface just one annoyance and she's a crazed menace.

WE DON'T ALL MIX YOU TWIT

She just left her boyfriend at my house as if everyone mixes well. That's hypnotism, social.

I'm scared to death of your friends and since you brought em around be gone, the end.

The Jezebel sister laid evil seeds in the target's new town who spread it around: CONTAGION.

SEPARATE MEANS HOLY

Better have bodyguards if you wanna say what you want. Be ready for attack every minute.

The only way to escape ageist comments of the rude is to go into isolation which is your heaven.

And then there was Mario the fat homosexual who ruined my rep from pure envy that's all.

And then there was Craig the whoremonger who went to Brawley twice a week the fat loser.

Sending FBI after parents is lunacy but Hitler was too yet assumed total control of a country.

Your biggest achievement is separation. Cut em all loose then celebrate your accomplishment.

Life in a small town was like a cat in a room full of rockingchairs for the sensitive avatar.

Dunning-Kruger was in full effect as the dumbed down liberal femmes in town mocked the Elect.

The more you cut loose the better off you'll be. They're wasting your time and precious liberty.

They waste time trying to figure out what they mean as they constantly interrupt the queen.

MORE TROUBLE THAN THEY'RE WORTH

You wanna get me on the phone so you can bloviate but I won't give you a chance again mate.

It's so boring hearing about all the people you're meeting. Hey Mr. Butterfly what about me?

They ask you a question, you spend time writing it out then they ignore it as if they forgot.

SEPARATE MEANS HOLY

They're too narcissistic to go deep or reply back when it doesn't serve, no conversation, no verve.

The better we are in the present the more astonishing the past looks when held back by kooks.

It's just easier to get huge donations from woke corporations than it is to truly listen.

HIX POLITIX UPDATES

A racist praises every country but his own. This reminds us of AOC, Pelosi and Trudeau.

Exterminist antisemitism in the soul of German people from time immemorial--or was it social?

Lesson from president or school board: "sit down, shut up and take it--you don't have the power."

Critical Race Theory is the Hate Whitey Program. It's not just sick/morally wrong it's a sham.

Joe isn't a sweet empathic gentleman he's a cold ruthless politician who would do anything man.

An infrastructure bill should be about highways, waterways & bridges not the left's pet projects.

California's oil spill reflects everything else going on in that democrat socialist progressive hell.

"Show me the man and I'll find you the crime". L. Beria, Chief of Soviet Secret Police.

School Board fallacies: we don't like their politics so they don't deserve civil liberties.

There's a twisted hate of the unvaxxed by the established state who wants to dictate.

SEPARATE MEANS HOLY

First of all it was a liberal town, who needs that--I hated it. Second of all they hated conservatives.

PEOPLE WASTE YOUR TIME

You're only young once & also only old once. Both have advantages so live em to the fullest.

It's based on hard work not image-magic from millions of pictures of the false self's tricks.

I hate phones. Simultaneity cancels each other out and you gotta listen to bloviation a lot.

Anything you gotta say you can say in an email then I have a record & answer when I want to.

People wanna bloviate on all the people they met and honestly I cannot stand that, so get.

If one dumps you cuz you won't talk on the phone it's a wonderful sieve and be glad he's gone.

Cuz he just wants to go and on how great he is and all the friends he has. He's a loser, an ass.

CHOSEN AS A VESSEL

I don't know why God chose me as the vessel for this Creative Act. I died then He brought me back.

Just to face public opprobrium--like Van Gogh or Beethoven--was a horrible burden to overcome.

Why I'm a happy lifelong isolate: they're pathologically envious and I'm pathologically shy.

You don't have to prove yourself to them. You'd do them much better just disappearin/allow imaginin'.

SEPARATE MEANS HOLY

In a normal world everyone has boundaries. But not in Borrego Springs, everyone knew your business.

WANTING PRIVACY IS AN AFFRONT

Just wanting to pull back, not be included or isolate was taken as an affront, a rejection and insult.

You can tell a social culture by the architecture: Front door on street/no fence between you and them.

I shudder looking back to what it was like having to adapt to a liberal social culture of low intellects.

They brought on the black cloud, we mal-adapted thru addictive devices to cope without God.

It's not an outer reality it's an INNER. They feel strength in numbers so it's all social but you're the winner.

30 years in the desert in total obscurity overcoming the Dunning-Krugers in town while finding God.

I may need you soon. Let's see who's available when that call goes out as it always does in human life.

Can you believe the ironic truth that the BEST saints were the worst sinners? Yes, I said the WORST.

Yes, I can sense what you're up to when I'm not around. That's why I pull back at times you clown.

DUNNING-KRUGER: DUMB THINKING THEY'RE SMART

What is the Dunning-Kruger? It's the dumb thinking they're smart--most dangerous for sure.

What messed us up? The influence of other people. With trauma we swallow them whole/mimic evil.

SEPARATE MEANS HOLY

I may need you soon. Get ready to relocate to a safe place of exquisite beauty with the theoretical ace.

Of course I can't talk to you it wouldn't be right. I communicate thru signs and symbols, aye.

You must fight the feeling that you're at your end. Like Churchill said it's the **BEGINNING** of the end.

Women. Even the nice ones will turn on you when they get the upper hand, it's the Jezebel spirit in them.

When I go to his office we do what he wants. When he comes to my office we do what he wants.

Cleanse your memory, it should all be white as snow. No matter what you did it's all the same you know.

We all have skeletons in the closet, don't air your dirty laundry. These expressions come in handy.

Tho' they offer help they're just trying to barge into the house. Worm their way in, that's how it is.

It's home. Treating it carelessly is one thing but turning it into a cheap roadhouse for strangers is another.

It's all about self-justification, inability to take responsibility and blame-shifting to maintain identity.

No your boyfriend can't stay here while you go lollygagging around. This isn't a pit-stop it's my **HOME**.

You're just gonna leave him here and i'm supposed to be a hostess? You don't know if people can mix!

SOCIAL IS NOT GODLY

I went thru the same thing with all the churches: Them thinking socials were the same as goodness.

SEPARATE MEANS HOLY

You give her a taste outa the stew pot and then put the spoon back in the pot? Are you kidding you nut?

We're supposed to worship God not people. We're told to love God first THEN our neighbor tho' evil.

Since WWII the social has overtaken urges for independence and we're told to love people first tho' dunces.

You gotta forgive because otherwise what are you gonna do, go and yell at someone in a rest home?

I've done so many crazy things it had to be some demon working in me it was so outlandish/unfree.

Once you accept your own unexplained outbursts and insanities you get a little more forgiving see?

That guy you've a crush on will NOT be the one for you and you'll find your true love with the NEXT one.

At first it may hurt to see the wild wickedness of people but it's so profitable--the only way to security.

I had no idea in the collective unconscious I'd see demons or feel emotions deeper/darker than the oceans.

It's not a matter that I'm a goodie two shoes but I don't wanna face God's wrath again, I love living wholesome.

MUST KNOW THY HISTORY

I really think knowing your history is more important than naming all the plants, flowers, stars, whatever.

Knowing your history is a matter of respect for those who died to give you this life to your benefit.

It's not morbid curiosity, don't you see? It's this: did they die for nothing cuz we never knew the tragedy?

SEPARATE MEANS HOLY

How could she be so cold as to not be interested in "getting all absorbed" in this historical catastrophe?

Are you kidding? MILLIONS died, and she doesn't wanna hear about it? I can't believe my ears/eyes.

Women wanna learn the names of flowers, trees, mushrooms but never the real, heartbreaking truths too.

He's a cult of personality but you've got solid work under your belt honey and that's the winner eventually.

God, when i'm dead there will be no more memory so why be plagued by them now? Dear Lord it's awful

MY HOME IS NOT YOUR PIT STOP

This is my HOME not a pit stop for you and your friends. At least call first but better yet, good riddance.

To come without calling is such an insult, you think I'm just waiting for you like a sitting duck?

Old age sux when you get to the point where solid foods causes acid reflux but on soups life takes off.

The fact that she disappeared suddenly--was that your fault or hers? Was she not reacting to a jerk?

This is my HOME not your laundromat. Here I'll give you two quarters for the one down the block you nut.

This is my HOME not a place to charge your phone. You waste my precious time and I just wanna be alone.

You. come to see ME not use me for everything in my home that is handy. Get some respect you hippie.

BAD ASSOCIATIONS AND YOU

SEPARATE MEANS HOLY

I can't take your channel anymore, it gets puerile or pointless at times and I can't wade thru it, no more time.

And that includes everyone associated with you, apparently. It's birds of a feather--you're all boring actually.

With INFINITE things to interest me you think I'd waste any more time with thee? Not with this treachery.

It was a drastic departure: from keep your hands off my stuff to SHARING: what's mine is yours/horrifying.

It's possible to be brilliant and crazy at the same time. When whole we become wise instead, a rare find.

SCAPEGOAT SYNDROMES

When a whole town or tribe projects its shadow onto one that's called the scapegoat syndrome, amen.

All their dirty little secrets they can't face they project onto one as if she's the reason for all their problems.

Dad, Grandad and Great Grandad wrote in quips like me but didn't have the hurts--the Ph.D. in the Streets.

Listen you crazy marching girls: It was white males who ended slavery all over the world.

It's you people pushing the racist crap who are racist and it's getting old-- using division as a tool for control.

"LOVE TRUMPS HATE" MEANS F-YOU

"Love trumps hate" actually means "F-you! by brainwashed idiots.

Poli-Psyche: The study of how groups are manipulated and brainwashed, creating disasters and fuss.

She is superficial, stupid, knows nothing, shallow: The most popular girl is loved by cowards, the yellow.

SEPARATE MEANS HOLY

Radical feminists hate men of any type. They yell "love trumps hate"--yikes!

The female marchers make a big display of their mental illness. Vicious, malicious, vacuous: God help us!

They keep doubling down on evil thinking they'll defeat us but are destroying themselves in front of us.

Trump wants a beautiful, happy world. Obama said "you can't have cars, you can't have air conditioning"--grrrr.

It's not hateful to say "you're not a citizen so you don't come and get all this stuff free"—do you see?

Crazy feminists and leftists will become increasingly irrelevant so don't worry about them, but be adamant.

The government does not attract the brightest/the best--the innovators uncomfortable as "regulators".

Many think the devil is so cool. But he's fallen and weak so why wear him on your clothes, you fools?

We're made in the image of God so why follow the devil who is so weak, ugly, puny, ineffectual and evil?

They are made mentally ill by MSN and it's declassified the CIA did it to them.

HE'S KILLING UNELECTED SECRET GOVERNMENT

Donald Trump was killing corporate, unelected, secret world government. We should all thank God, amen!

Major technology companies and gun manufacturers are returning to the U.S. big time (guns aren't a crime)!

He's done hundreds of things--massive car manufacturers coming back and no just walking across the border.

SEPARATE MEANS HOLY

We asked for it, God gave it to us. Donald Trump is the wrecking ball of the New World Order, or bust!

Because they transferred so much power to the executive (illegally) he can just get loads done! Hah!

They put out such trash but God uses evil for good against them.

Liberalism is a mental illness and I was one of them I guess.

The attempt to delegitimize Trump by the media is in fact delegitimizing the media and I love it America!

Things are happening so fast there is no way I can do anything but watch, study and report--what a sport!

The media's had monopoly so long, they're mad as hell! What a joy to watch them self-destruct as they rebel.

Watch the press conferences--the left is so disoriented they don't know how to cover them, not a chance.

Lie, upon lie, upon lie by the democrats--unchecked for years. haha, go ahead, show me your tears!

Hah: We don't have to do a thing now but sit back and watch them destroy themselves with lies and false "facts".

What the media saw as a "funeral march" we saw as a country waking up, so refreshing and relieving, yup!

WOMEN'S MARCH OF SORE LOSERS

The women's march was actually the "sore losers" march--because, what were they protesting about?

If crazy women love Islam and wanna wear a beekeeper's suit so much, let em go to the middle east--good luck!

To the deluded mainstream media, anything which is not far left, is far right--Hitlerian, fascist, a blight.

SEPARATE MEANS HOLY

Hitler's Nazi Party was actually far left so they don't know what they're talking about as it's expressed.

The leftist media got away with lies for years cuz they were an echo chamber but that's all over.

Don't waste your precious God-given energy arguing with the left (they're daft, you're not) or be bereft.

Arrest Obama for treason--we've got hundreds of reasons!

They call "fake news" any disagreement with the liberal agenda.

So self-evident, but not to the left!

Next Trumpism: Chemtrails (geo-engineering) approved in 1992.

Trump supporters have an immediate connection: feel it.

The left believes it's unhappy because of us--classic projection.

The left says "any stock market surge is Hitler"—two trillion cuza Trump but he's a killer? go figure

Hillary's crimes were so big she thought "too big to fail" or "if gonna steal, steal big" but Trump will avail.

Russia's gonna bring back organic farming--it flips a switch in humans, we're meant to do it, proven.

Farmers are the toughest, it's true Americana (vs. the city sluggish) and they love Trump, the mostess.

FEMINISTS ARE DANGEROUS

Trump was nice to Hillary cuz she's dangerous. Before you kill em, shake the hand of mafia or it's hazardous.

You'll be used as examples of what scum traitors are for decades. Delusional media: sick/evil in spades.

SEPARATE MEANS HOLY

Hillary, Madonna and other harpies are opposite to the beauty of full womanhood. Twisted, spoiled goods.

Old guard conceded every major issue so they wouldn't be called names by the left and this created a mess.

I'm done with FOX. Despite a good few it's filled with liberal speedbumps that make it a bore and a lie (it sux).

When it comes to sexy ads, feminists and Islamist want the same thing: ban them--and this is accelerating.

Casting out reason/logic for favor: Identity Politics isn't fair but that's what we see from govs to mayors.

Replacing principal for ego and personal identity. That's what we've witnessed and it's a real legal tragedy.

It's disturbing the mythologizing of campus rape culture and the wage gap yet impervious to reason and fact.

FOX: It's like the truth is not enough: they gotta be engaging, charming, funny and all that fancy stuff.

Mis-reporting for ideological reasons does far more damage to America than Trump's foibles here and there.

Progressive left were in power but forgot how to argue. So we see strange definitions of things unaltered.

The peculiar nonsensical slogans they're shouting having no arguments of any value: aggravating.

FEMINISM AND OTHER LIBERAL SCAMS

Left bullied us to believe global warming rather than persuasion so we don't buy it at all: be gone.

Feminists aren't concerned with rapes in Islam but rather mansplaining, manspreading and microaggressions.

SEPARATE MEANS HOLY

Like Islam, feminism spreads like cancer and soon the body breaks down. He says anything, she frowns.

Make up crimes of white college men but ignore rapes of the brown as feminists crush speech all around.

If liberals call you names rest assured you've said something right. They can't think, no reason/logic, a blight.

There are some racists around but not many.

For generations females blamed for men's passions--saying "cover up" rather than men controlling em.

The liberals are so invested in identity politics their head explodes just at the thought of a gay conservative.

Progressive left has completely colonized entertainment, the media and academia and it's all against America.

Feminism is cancer. Milo Yiannopoulos

Feminism: Everything that goes wrong is the fault of a man or patriarchy.

We live in so much confusion women bark if you open the door. Milo

4 out of five women don't identify as feminists though 85% see sexes as equal (should feel relief at this info).

Statistically the dumbest become social justice warriors. Can't cut it so they claim victimhood of course.

MALE BASHING AND WHITE TRASHING

White men are endlessly demeaned and ridiculed from every avenue, some react with self-hate, have you?

Third wave feminism on the campuses: idea of a mysterious force keeping them down ("men are asses").

SEPARATE MEANS HOLY

Male-bashing is born out of spite, meanness, pettiness and is buttressed by the globalist plan to finish us.

Does anyone doubt that feminists are vindictive? Or are they altruistic saints, pure and unaddicted?

The sea hags will be defeated.

Do feminists gossip behind your back, do they backstab? Are you afraid of calumny from all their gab?

I had a feminist friend once. She talked about me all over town, competitive and obviously wanted me down.

Men are beginning to apologize for living. I always say "you have nothing to be sorry for"--it's from feminism.

Vulnerable college women being told lies by feminists to explain their shortcomings: they stop trying.

Men told they must become sensitive (to feminism) so take on stilted roles of the false self: wimpism.

Most self-hating creature: male feminist who ends up reversing into the opposite role of being a sadist.

As feminists get older they're either painfully embarrassed for early behavior or even more jaded and ill-favored.

Men are made to feel guilty for the "rape culture" that doesn't exist. Except by Muslims who women won't dis.

Many women tried to "copy men" and became promiscuous. Not that men are, it's just exposed as that.

WOMEN ENCOURAGED TO DIVORCE

Many women fought back not with fists but affairs and divorce. Imagine all the broken homes and hearts.

SEPARATE MEANS HOLY

A terrible and pervasive sexism aimed at men, to destroy our world with out defense.

"Reverse racism isn't real" but if you're a white guy you're the devil.

They wear it like a badge of honor--virtue signaling that they're a "feminist". They can't see the ugly gist.

You coulda ended hooked to a feminist, thank God you avoided that mess.

We won and there's nothing they can do about it! Never forget that to stay way way way way above it.

Bullies can dish it out but can't take it--that's their characteristic.

Liberals want to control every darn thing. If it exists they wanna fix it and this attitude wrecks everything.

He's just doing all the things he said he would.

They get away with fake news--making stuff up, screw jobs--because they can.

Barry O. ripped this country apart and it's bleeding still. The left will be protesting for months/overkill.

The embarrassing virtue signaling about how good they are: That's what the left has always used especially stars.

Trump was elected in the greatest upset victory in American history. We don't care what you want, hippies.

Some religions don't teach peace/love but to kill the infidel, or it's ok to rape children after capturing a cell.

LIBERALISM IS A MENTAL DISORDER

Liberalism is a mental disorder. Liberals aren't known for logic but emotion: if it feels good do it forever.

SEPARATE MEANS HOLY

Trump is the doctor: you may not like results and the inoculation isn't fun but you'll thank him in the long run.

A small minority is attacking Trump for doing what we put him in to do—proceed, while those you eschew.

Barry is gone, Donny is here. It feels real good to have a new sheriff who does what's right though they smear.

Trump: Shots heard around the world to tyrants and smug intelligentsia-- we've had it, be gone with ya.

Don't patronize left wing fanatics like Starbucks who wanna hire 10,000 immigrants but not us Americans!

The damage Barry O. has done to this country will last many years and that's why Trump's in high gear.

Demon rats who did this to us are now getting a taste of their own medicine which we endured back then.

You can't change the mind of those who have no mind. Michael Savage

Liars Hillary and Barry raised their ugly traitor heads--of course, we expected that from the walking dead.

It's been a party for em but parties always come to an end. Sooner or later, keg's empty and hangover begins.

The small minority is the loudest. Don't let that fool you for under Trump America will end up the proudest.

CURSE: ILLEGAL ALIENS COME FIRST

They took the money from old people and veterans lying in the gutter and gave it to illegal aliens for a starter.

Big church groups living off the taxpayer and bringing invaders in will now go out of business: good bye then.

SEPARATE MEANS HOLY

Barry did such a number on you and you even voted twice. You were so in love with him (brains of mice).

You were so in love with Barry you didn't even care what he did! How disgusting justifying the sordid.

You just wanna stop Trump, not terrorism.

Screaming cuss words and talking about body parts: this is third wave feminism--insanity off the charts.

We've been under the boot of leftist autocrats for so long we forgot how good it could be: through Trump, set free!

With Trump every day is Christmas and it doesn't get any better. Pamela Geller

We love Trump cuz he speaks for us: He's the voice of the voiceless (called nuts).

Look at children of the democrats (suicide, drugs) and compare that to first family (charm, grace) of Trump!

Do not make perfect the enemy of the good. Trump is great and you're the "low info" with hearts of wood.

They lie to advance their narrative--look at Obamacare, so incredibly abusive.

America is now the scene of political violence in response to ideas. Milo

The federal government is compelled by fed law to punish sanctuary cities by withdrawing funds: hah.

VIOLENCE IS INTEGRAL TO LEFTIST VIEW

Violence is an integral part of the leftwing view. Their only vision is "burn it down, baby". Michael Savage

It's sinking in that they lost so they're becoming desperate and we can see their violent true selves.

SEPARATE MEANS HOLY

The socialist dictatorship of the most corrupt regime in history (California) refused to stop the violence.

California loves the anarchy cuz it keeps people's eye off the money they're stealing. Need the marines, really.

Trump threatens to cut federal funding to UC Berkeley after a night of violence. Good for you, do please.

Trump said if no free speech and unstopped violence on innocent people then no federal funds. Fun!

They don't know how gov works nor do they care. They are only self-aggrandizing so Trump, beware!

The vast majority of billionaires are left-wing hippies who want to keep the middle class poor/downstairs.

There's nothing new with anarchy and obstructionism is middle name of democrats, AKA "by any means necessary".

It's been going on at Berkeley, just more inflamed. These things always accelerate, nothing stays the same.

Students are encouraged by faculty and rich dems like Pelosi to "shut it down" and "protest in streets", crazy.

The Free Speech Movement started in 1965 with the hippies but not for the right wing speakers like you/me.

They're not only ideologically but also morally bankrupt while saying we should be more civil and tolerant!

Environmental groups: left wing advocacy orgs with every trendy issue in the same basket (gays, trans, you got it).

LEFT HAS NO OBJECTION TO CHAOS

Left has no objection to chaos: they accept Jihad and the disasters coming from it but Trump will fight it.

SEPARATE MEANS HOLY

Feminism is the default setting for college age women but it makes them mean, nasty, vindictive vermin.

What man would want them? You gotta subscribe to the natural order eventually: birds and bees in sum.

What men want is the sweet little lady. Where are they? Crazy, freaky, some brainy but most are shady.

The democrats are telling illegals how to resist the border patrol: They just want anarchy, votes and civil war.

Universities won't fight back but nature abhors a vacuum and it'll come against and destroy them: fact.

The cycles of seasons, moons, empires, nations and peoples: They rise and they fall but now we're shirking evil.

Liberals don't want us to investigate voter fraud, of course not.

Big business hated Donald Trump and loved Hillary but that's changing.

"My job is to make sure they get that they have privilege"

It's a culture war. To see what that is see Hollywood scum at their events then listen to media for more.

They feel superior without doubt.

EDUCATION THE GREATEST WEAPON

Education is a weapon whose effects depend on who holds it in his hands and at whom it is aimed. Charlotte Iserbyt

A landslide though only one-third of conservatives voted: The tip of the spear so keep that well-noted.

If we can't convince them how they're conned, there is no hope. Tell em though you're banned/called a dope.

Suppression only makes us stronger.

SEPARATE MEANS HOLY

Corrupt media's against Trump cuz they're owned by multi-national corps who want us poor so they can rob.

Obama's encouraging protestors to continue the violence. Scary stuff, the ideologues are tireless.

Liberals can't see danger cuz their conscience is seared from their true nature so they love the stranger.

They can't renege and accept Trump cuz then they're admitting what fools they've been and this they can't lump.

We didn't elect you to "reach across the aisle" but to do an agenda which comes against the vile.

Trump didn't "fail" he's just not appointing your guys. You lost, you failed so accept it/repent for your lies.

Is there anyone more irrelevant than Glenn Beck right now, saying God told him to vote for Cruz? Wow

What about the poor folk who are already here? Liberals call them "bitter clingers" cuz aliens they fear.

Liberals down on USA know nothing about what other countries are like. They are so lucky, but they fight.

Indoctrinating very small children--despicable crime. You won't believe what they're telling them, the slime.

IDIOCRACIES GET WORSE THEN DIE

They're telling tiny young kids to kill the racist Trump. This after expelling them for making finger guns.

Liberalism will now become more and more irrelevant and the divisions will get larger as they vent.

Idiocracy: literally everything has to be part of the social justice movement.

SEPARATE MEANS HOLY

In the decadent late stages of society, bizarre behavior proliferates and is legitimized, fetishizing pathology.

When ugliness is venerated as beauty we know we're in the depraved late stages of civilization.

Pop culture is a threat to the west since it provides our enemies with a justifiable reason to destroy us.

Safe spaces, PC, virtue signaling, gender studies: When did "being cool" become parroting stupidities?

Share: Popular culture does NOT represent western civilization--only the great works like Beethoven.

By making our cultural underpinnings completely meaningless (Miley Cyrus) it is easily overthrown and dissed.

Popular culture is so invasively vulgar it's seen as the reason for terror attacks making us suffer.

Leave empty cultural Marxism for Renaissance: beauty, talent and exalting human accomplishment.

The herd mentality without a mind, united as one kind: hating Trump and blind.

Trump doesn't care: He knows he's doing the right thing so let em lie and make stuff up but he'll stay in prayer.

A black person is 2000 x more likely to be killed by another black, than a white/cop/KKK--that's a fact.

TRUMPSTERS NEED PROTECTION

If you're a Donald Trump supporter you must stay very close to the police: You are a marked man of peace.

It's the same spirit in all us patriots: it's God wanting us to have justice.

Judges aren't supposed to "help people" but interpret the law of good vs. evil.

SEPARATE MEANS HOLY

Our guy is so strong and smart! He suffered/broke through the log jam of bought off media and hard hearts.

The no-action let-em-burn-it-down university is a criminal enclave. It's about to change/they will behave.

Universities now devil worshippers and death lovers: not the whole generation but can goodness be recovered?

You're not paranoid thinking they're out to get you (please!) or those trying to change the world are evil enemies.

Youth: Unable to diffuse anger into music or subculture they turn to the mental ghetto of identity politics.

The pressure to conform to canons of popular taste--or lack of taste--has never been stronger. PJ Watson

Lincoln had federal judges arrested and the best presidents put them down.

Fake polls: left-leaning means lying.

Once we absorb degeneracy our moral filters are irreparably damaged. PJ Watson

Cultural hypersexualization normalizes cheating and betrayal--when everyone else is doing it, it's less shameful.

We love Trump cuz we're sick of being bullied by the word police and love how he said what he pleased.

It's not "see you later, we won" but now we gotta protect our man so he can protect us--we've only begun.

Prepare for the rough months ahead too because Trump's gonna continue to do what he said he'd do.

The Clinton Foundation is the largest unprosecuted charity fraud in the history of mankind. Charles Ortel

POP CULTURE REFLECTIONS

SEPARATE MEANS HOLY

The pope likens "conspiracies" to the sexual desire for feces. Not a catholic but a Jesuit communist, jeez.

Left calls Trump "ineffectual" though he's gotten more done in 2 weeks then 8 year under pseudo-intellectuals.

It wasn't that you were an ass in your past but you lacked self so reflected pop culture (no class).

Quit arguing with liberals for what does it help? Save your energy and withdraw into your happy sane self.

Why we love him: Though the press hates him he's completely unencumbered by popular opinion.

Liberals heads are spinning right now. Gaga didn't trash Trump but just stuck to her job and entertained.

Liberals bash GaGa cuz she didn't bash Trump.

Backlash: She dared to not attack Trump.

Filthy pop culture is last stage of civilization decline, but repentance brings us back like Nineveh (refined).

Trumpism: It's a badge of honor if the leftist press hates him.

Media has a marginalization agenda. Trump

Liberals think all cultures are alike/equal but there's nothing more false: some are good and some are evil.

SOCIAL HYPNOTISM OF HERDS/TRIBES

It's "social hypnotism": how cultures think alike. It's like a herd or flock of birds in perfect unison/flight.

Split between left and right is growing daily. A wide chasm and there's no going back, like a Muslim and an Israeli.

SEPARATE MEANS HOLY

I'm never arguing with them again. It made me sick and fatigued back then so I'll just talk to smart friends.

Stress comes from arguing with idiots so get healthy by avoiding the hideous, oblivious, lascivious and pitiless.

All negative polls are fake news. DJ Trump

Our guy thrives in mayhem and uses it to his own advantage, amen!

To be prepared for war is one of the most effectual means of ensuring peace. George Washington

These people are like dumbed down wild animals. There is no reasoning with them and they are implacable.

Trump's not moving fast enough--hurry up, roll it all out!

The media is a nonstop barrage of negative news about our president.

Where the left sees "discrimination" the right sees "safety and protection".

Sitcoms throw entire programming into leftist indoctrination. Putting down fathers and moms up, fornication.

Liberals heads are spinning right now. Gaga didn't trash Trump but just did her job and entertained us all.

They said "he says outrageous things" but everything he said rang true to me--like a bell that rings.

The very tribe lost without you may ban you cuz they have that to learn: appreciation of all and why you do.

Dems would rather keep failed policies in place then put a qualified person in to do what we want, ok?

President wants to keep us safe but the fake news says "it's all ok--there are NO terrorist attacks, no way."

CHILDISH DEMOCRATS LOSING LUSTER

SEPARATE MEANS HOLY

Childish democrats are quickly losing luster: Delay, run the clock out, not come to hearings, filibuster.

The left favors feel good sentiment over safety, guilt assuagement over decency.

Trump'll smash political correctness, safe spaces and trigger warning culture and liberate us from the vulgar.

The right is all about safety, the left: "let em all in" and it will always be that way though obviously wrong ok?

Trump: even one killed is too much. Left: don't stereotype, don't judge!

How powerful standing up in a room full of leftists and spew libtard platitudes to applause while being rude.

Safety precautions are now "mean spirited" rather than just common sense in this generation (so dense).

See the past as "the war". It was your mal-adaptation to liberalism, a mental illness leaving you scarred and poor.

The social hypnotism of liberalism lays groundwork for abortions, divorces, addictions, heresies, debaucheries.

We have to forgive em (they were possessed by social hypnotism to believe a lie) but many were hurt, oh my.

Every hurt, every evil memory comes down to "liberalism is a sickness" and I must remember this, then diss.

All states are different and some are riddled through and through with liberalism. Move for exhilarating escapism.

Been through so much with the election and now this: people are quitting the news now--it's all dissed.

TWO AMERICAS: CRAZY COASTS VS. HAPPY FARMERS

SEPARATE MEANS HOLY

There are two Americas: the crazy coasts and the happy holy farmers in the middle, the guideposts.

Social hypnotism can consume a state till everyone you meet's a liberal or justice warrior filled with hate.

My war was California liberalism while not realizing it, thinking it was me. Then moved to Utah/feel so free!

The left is organizing fight clubs to go out and kill "nazis" which is you, me, us.

University of California is trying to divert attention from the looming pedophilia raids (e.g. Penn State).

To grow up in a sheltered religious household then exposed to and controlled by liberalism was so cold.

At UCI I was hit on by professors in the most crude ways--won't stop talking about it to the end of my days.

There's a cultural psychology to every state. Re-adaptation is your therapy as you geographically relocate.

Both coasts = crazy. Go inner, be happy.

Burning with with self-flattery they seek to keep us down. That's the nature of tyranny: hating the renowned.

They're hoping you don't want the fight but if you persist you'll win cuz they're little demons (low soul-height).

Fox is sneaky how they put down Trump. The Murdock sons are running things and they're liberals (crud).

HE FALLS IN MUD AND COMES BACK UP

Every time they say our guy falls down in the mud he always comes up smelling like roses twice as much!

Though they call him obnoxious, bombastic and irritating we love him.

SEPARATE MEANS HOLY

Even Michael Savage is putting our leader down--I'm turning em all off now.

Our guy has a heart. That's altogether different from the sadistic fake-nice of the apathetic (with smiles large).

They speak against Trump and I get sad. Then he snaps back—so bad--and I'm happy again, so glad!

The democrats were the slave owners and the KKK. They're mean spirited but covered by a "nice" identity.

He knows what we went through--he feels sympathy. So refreshing after experiencing cold smiling apathy.

If you trust Fox and suddenly they throw you a zinger against your winner it hurts, it's disconcerting, a bummer.

Divorces happening as libtard wives disgusted with Trumpist husbands. Good riddance, be gone hons'

Dems are choking on loser's tears, embarrassment, questioning, deflation, humiliation and self-effacement.

Leftists' rhetoric appeases their anti-Trump agenda at all cost, regardless that our safety is lost.

They're bringing themselves down. Arrogance before the fall, last ditch efforts, implosion/panic: clowns.

THE LEFT HATES ANOMALIES

They hate any anomaly like a conservative homosexual/black. No mental flex: don't fit the matrix, reject.

Overthrowing the bill of rights and the constitution is not free speech but outright illegal and sedition.

Piers Morgan knows he was defeated and is now crawling back acting like he's one of us the newly elited.

SEPARATE MEANS HOLY

Americans rejected your failed leftist policies and now you wanna obstruct plans of our elected president?

To Pocahontas and leftist friends: if you're judge-shopping and obstructing results in terrorism it's your end.

Trump has done what 4 presidents have but now it's a tragedy?

They never give up building a case against Trump (to not be seen as wrong) can you believe this stuff?

The amount of subversion against Trump is astounding, even leaking rats in the whitehouse are obstructing.

Trump studies everything all night long. He catches on, he always comes back/wins against the evil throng.

Get into politics so inferior men can't rule over you. That means to look good, be good, study and pray too

"He shouldn't criticize judges" when there've been arrests of supreme court justices all through the ages.

Stop listening/repeating their spiel. It's all bull, easily disproven, unreal.

End of phoniness: Elizabeth Warren (Pocahontas) getting on her high horse with pure race-baiting of course.

TWO-FACED FOX IS CACOPHONOUS

FOX: cacophonous, interruptive, frustrating, boring, aggravating! Few pearls interjected keeps ya comin'

Fake news: Not just omissions but wrong priorities, focus or trivializations

Comeback Trump: As dems sue his every move we must wait for his ever-win over those who disapprove.

We elected him for his sly smarts. Once aware he cleans house so hold on for great changes to start.

SEPARATE MEANS HOLY

Donald since they're gonna slam you for everything just ignore it all, do your thing

They put our lives at risk just for politics.

Ignore the anti-Trumpers cuz they're just paid protestors.

Soros pays big bux to make it look like Trump sux but it's all lies, he's deluxe.

Sickening stupidity of the arrogant confirmed by the money they make in their leftist liberal element.

It's a lie to omit, distort or de-prioritize focus but that's the leftist pundits in their verbal hocus-pocus.

They're making it look like the mentally ill protests are much bigger than they are. Plan: villainize our star.

People are so used to being pushed around mentally it's all about "agreement" and it's embarrassing.

Marriages are breaking up over Trump.

9th circus has 90% reversal rate. They're the ones who outlawed U.S. flag shirts--arrest them like did Abe.

National sovereignty and the flag is now racism. That's how far we've gone into mental illness and barbarism.

Iranians shouting "death to America" aligned with the left against Trump: think about that--aren't they crud?

Trump is not like Hitler. Just because a leader wants order doesn't mean they're like a dictator. Marion Andrews

GENDER OFFENDERS

Why aren't feminists fighting for mutilated Pakistani women? We're so lucky to have gentle American men.

SEPARATE MEANS HOLY

Micro aggressions aren't coming to your gender but lack of refinement and class: be a lady not an ass.

Tradition has it Obama will always be called "president" but for all his crimes he should be arrested.

The Christian life is a wonderful exciting journey despite these treacheries.

California wants money. Trump: shut down sanctuary cities, deport illegals and fight campus violence honey.

Libs outraged that Ivanka wore the dress she made, but not that the Clinton Foundation paid and played?

A society that cannot defend its children has no future. Vladimir Putin

Just love God, no more tears: I learned this in a tiny cabin on one thousand acres in the desert wilderness for 27 years.

They didn't know any better. They were swept up into fear-laden PC culture so forgive these vultures.

What the man has promised he's done so shut up libs he's only begun.

Transgender suicide rate is 40%. Go against biology = torment.

People who kill people should be killed but babies who are innocent should not.

Faulty thinking: taking the marginal case and applying it to all. Abortion's not about rape/incest, that's small.

BLIND CULTURAL RELATIVISM

Today's democrats are immature, entitled and crazy--yet to grow up.

We've fought too long to be pulled back by small jealous women too limited to comprehend our advances. Judge Jeanine

Because of our blind cultural relativism we had to have millions here for a season but now they'll be leavin'.

SEPARATE MEANS HOLY

25% of all college students have been diagnosed with a mental disorder. A giant brainwashing facility, horror.

Save your money and don't send kids to college. Fake degrees, no jobs and messed up with no knowledge.

Being diagnosed gives them a license to not study, work, succeed and that's their victimhood identity.

Diagnoses are awards that change status or expectations towards.

A pharmaceutical force has taken over the young and given rise to insane behavior courtesy of big pharma.

Being over-diagnosed prevents them from going through rites of passages and growth. Crisis, synthesis, rise above.

Colleges are pharmaceutically controlled: psychiatric clinics and captives of the pharma cartel--it's cold.

The fact that so many hate Trump explains why I've felt so outa sync

Overwhelming but with Trump things change--the sea parts--and there's a comeback as he punts over them.

They'll even drop friends who don't share their hatred of Trump.

Become a Trump-hater just to join the club or not be snubbed--what a dud.

LIBS FELT SUPERIOR FOR FOUR DECADES

They felt superior for so long being a part of this liberal thing there is no way they could be proven wrong.

The more people believe it the less it's true.

Fake supermen: not fighting bad guys but fighting for "good" nonetheless.

Prosperity makes monsters, adversity makes men. Alex Jones

SEPARATE MEANS HOLY

Soros bankrolled anti-Trump protests--just point out the fraud then reject.

Losers stay arrogant but shaky--can't accept it, get more flaky.

They want to extinguish thinkers--a bright light in a room full of vampires.

Elites are throwing everything they've got against Trump.

Being so immature they can't get straight but continue to push, harass, violently protest, aggravate, bait.

It's solitude vs. social.

Obama was nice on surface but devil underneath (this they can't see) while Donald is just himself, free.

To face how wrong they are on Trump would mean to face how wrong an entire generation was--they can't!

Patriots need to street-preach liberty, bill of rights and constitution now.

Anti-Trump fervor: hysterical derangement.

Emptiness seeks company, fullness is distracted and bored by it: wants solitude for richness/profundity.

MASS MENTAL ILLNESS IN LIBERAL CULTURES

Crazy in, crazy out. If the dominant culture is liberal we adapt through mental illness without a doubt.

Insanity is a mal-adaptation to liberalism.

"It's all good" means "there is no justice" and that unnerves the righteous to the core so many seek solace.

To face what Hillary is is to face who they have been as hippies.

Clouded by dogma they can't see--like Merkel ruining her country.

Fascistic dogma systems are more like clubs, the mentality of mobs.

SEPARATE MEANS HOLY

Virtue signaling (act out goodness) comes off stilted like fake news.

We cannot allow a minority of people to hold a viewpoint that terrorizes the majority. Hillary Clinton

Since liberalism was the default setting in society and schools, conservatives were the minority, very un-cool.

The mainstream media is the enemy, Trump's poll #s are surging cuz we all know the media is deceiving.

He'll make rich those who bitch then we'll unify in the American niche.

I know the truth so why study all the detractors? Return to the moment for it's YOUR great life that matters.

The party line is not legit: To fit hate Trump, hate Trump and you fit.

I like Milo (he's an intellectual) but why must he say such dirty things? Bad example by a Christian.

Don't study Trump detractors anymore. Life's too short/a waste of precious time: He won and they're a bore.

Liberals are so ideologically committed, rabid and terrified of the future they can't accept our new leader.

You don't wanna talk to me cuz I'm so much smarter and I prove all your false narratives wrong. Owen Shroyer

I HAVE A RIGHT TO OFFEND YOU

I have a right to offend you under the first amendment.

They're fast to police conservatives and slow to police progressives.

Sin is a mal-adaptive coping device in dense environments.

Price-payoff systems: People repent of the sin when the price becomes too high for the payoff--hitting bottom.

SEPARATE MEANS HOLY

Liberalism: all-bull easily disproven but it can mess up your life for decades as society's default setting.

Liberalism is a religion with mantras. All bull, easily disproven but they'll kill you if you question it or mutter.

Feminists complain about "mansplaining" (yet they have it so good) while ignoring Islamic women and raping.

Fake news: I don't give em a chance to disappoint me like that--it's always like a stab in the back.

Trump: In 30 days more small business success than in 25 years.

Left is losing so will be increasingly violent. That's the dregs: vehement.

Whenever the left is vulnerable/going to get caught, they blame you for what they did. Loving: not.

The ineffectual are now aced out.

Left is face of disdainful superiority and virtue-signaling, but as they're aced out there's a quickening!

Fake news is trying to ruin our future, make us poor and divide the country more.

The spirit of 1776: Christ is the fulcrum, God is the father and the Holy Spirit is the delivery system. Alex Jones

Ideologues are always afraid of truth and thus they must banish it

A DARK WORLD WITH NO FREE SPEECH

Once free speech is gone your world turns dark with no escape.

Right to criticize and offend is the bulwark of western democracy.

Propaganda media vs. America

SEPARATE MEANS HOLY

The media did not create Donald Trump and they can't destroy him. Rush Limbaugh

Liberalism has been the default setting since the sixties and these are the grandchildren of the hippies.

He didn't "delegitimize" the press--they did it to themselves.

Media's losing ratings as everything they say is Trump-hating.

We hate the media cuz it's so biased and corrupt.

If everything they say/do/create is based on Trump-hate they'll be out of grace (disgraced) while we ace.

If you just talk issues, he's fine. But if you attack he becomes a pit bull--what a wonderful president of mine!

Trumpism reneged on every value someone under 35 had: Total trauma was the result and they're still mad.

Milo you're not a conservative since we are down-home family people guarding ears of children, you villain.

I had Stockholm Syndrome--caved when they pulled me down, gutted my identity: I was empty and unrenowned.

They always show their immaturities on TV so don't worry we'll win eventually.

I don't care Milo what you say, you said that horror was all-ok.

Milo made remarks in his lectures to tempt boys in the audience to sleep with him. Not a conservative, friends!

Warning: The losers are so immature they can't accept it/may get violent.

The enemedia is dead: long live the people.

Stop your shameless virtue signaling about how progressive you are.

MEDIA: THE FAKE BECOME RANK

SEPARATE MEANS HOLY

The media can turn on or off an entire culture. If fake we become rank, If saints we prosper/break the bank.

Instead of living in utopian vision you gotta be prepared for what could happen.

Let the First lady be the new model of the superior woman supplanting the feminist avatar which is ugly.

In media (gov) complex people with logic are driven out--only party-liners remain.

Americans don't care about whiny, privileged multi-millionaire players' (brats) tiresome virtue signaling.

I was hammered mercilessly, made fun of, marginalized. John Moore

Like health, happiness is an earned state.

The spoiled child given no boundaries becomes a demanding monster like the kids at Berkeley or others.

An earned state goes against our immediate pleasures in time until tastes and appetites are refined.

Reason for rules is to avoid negative consequences: remove the consequences, no more rules.

CONSEQUENCELESS HEDONISM

Despair of consequenceless hedonism: Irresponsibility is "self-expression" and self-restraint "repression".

You can't rebuild when all rules of self-restraint look like irrational neurotic repression, a mistake.

That's the world we live in, we're to accept this: everyone's a disease or victim in a Tower of Babble.

Follow the straight and narrow makes sense if you're walking on the beam not if just walking along, see?

SEPARATE MEANS HOLY

Our enemies are college professors and journalists. They are creating this absurd reality, what a mess.

We're being censured but take it as a complement. If afraid of our words it means we're dominant.

We're not haters, we have restraint. "Sexists, racists"--recall the 80's when mesmerized by Soul Train.

The blacks on Soul Train dressed beautifully and danced with ingenuity but now that's racist--really?

No sexism in the West but plenty in the East and Islam but with liberals that's never addressed.

They're painted a false reality like the whole country's in slavery and none of it's true believe me.

The immature minds, I don't blame them much. It's the strings behind the blind that are out to lunch.

We are quickly becoming post-Christian society and soon will be minority but still it's True Reality.

They just can't express anger without swearing and instantly their power is gone and it's boring.

They took young minds, which are idealistic/easily energized, and created communism disguised.

JP Rowling author of Harry Potter occult trend is pushing anti-depressants and grooming depression.

STRENGTH VS. BASKETCASE VICTIMS

Whatever doesn't kill you makes you stronger. They're turning you into absolute basketcase victims sir.

Churchhill was depressed but so focused with his job of saving the west he never caved into this test.

SEPARATE MEANS HOLY

They are the whiney millennial entitled society deserving of fame and fortune just for being born.

Anti-depressant usage up 400% over 20 years. It makes em wanna-be yes-people, zombies, careless.

50 years ago depression was "temporary unhappiness" not this lifelong illness for big pharma bucks.

Labeling Theory: You've bought the big lie and even let em poison you, making you a blank zombie.

In the frontier depression got you killed or starved. You had to work to stay alive, no time for that jive.

Depression label is the externalization that allows them to avoid responsibility for their life.

Depression: In all cases there's nothing wrong with brain just outlook in life and therapist directs strife.

One generation prospers and the next are debauched, neurotic, self-involved, hypnotized failures.

Psychiatry and profit motive: Keep em coming back. Many women fall for their therapist, that's a fact.

Depression comes from not being in the groove. Find out what you do best and it's all removed.

You are not a victim but they are telling you to surrender, take these pills and succumb.

CRIMINALIZATION OF POLITICAL DIFFERENCES

Criminalization of political differences endangers democracy. Alan Dershowitz

Liberals are not logical so just forget em, don't entangle--this is critical.

It's not that Milo's rude, but crude. Talking about sex too much sullies his message and intrudes.Top of Form

SEPARATE MEANS HOLY

Stop talking about sex Milo. You're destroying your worthy message and godly will see you as foe.

Milo says he's a victim not a defender of perversion, ok fine but why talk so dirty in conversations?

Kids may be sexualized but us elder Christians are not so kindly clean your speech of this perverse rot!

If you wanna know how to act/talk, emulate great grandmother cuz even grandmother may be rot.

It's been three generations of this crap so clean the slate to essentially: just your own map.

Churches must be totally protected to say "No, we're not marrying two men/two women, no way".

There's male and female, birds and the bees. There's no way you can re-organize this and stay free.

They act like this is all settled--it's not. We'll fight until the old paths are restored and we're rid of rot.

If they wanna settle down/build a life together, fine--a civil arrangement not churches forced in line.

Society is reorganized for the worst by crazy human rights courts.

WHERE ARE THE WHITE SUPREMACISTS?

Where are the "white supremacists"? We just wanna live our own lives but liberals create a nuisance.

This is you being devilish and crude not "unsayable truths".

Even though wrong, a movement explodes through youth throngs and just for kicks more come along.

First amendment means you have the right to argue about things without being called names.

SEPARATE MEANS HOLY

Antifa says the most victimized are the most legitimized, but the truth is: whites are most despised.

The more victimized the more legitimized so white males are at the bottom as the hated "privileged".

Value of opinion is based on group identity so if I don't like your ideas I'm attacking you personally?

Words are "micro-aggressions" attacking you personally. So you've a right to get violent at me?

You don't have to prove you're micro-aggressed, all that is required is your FEELING of offense.

The rich are not making you poor, they're paying your salary. Ben Shapiro

A generation of women have been told a baby's a polyp so they don't hate abortion or work to stop it.

A whole generation actually thinks it's not killing a child but removing a tumor: it's good, it's clever.

More they preach love, goodness, fairness the more violent we become: it's virtue signaling vs. the One.

IT'S A BABY NOT A POLYP

You can't prosecute them due to intent: They really think it's a polyp not a baby/they're made dense.

Forces in society vs. the individual trying to forge a way above the trends creating prevalent insanity.

Democracy is the worst system except for all the others. Winston Churchhill

Avoid lasciviousness. To know how to act think of great-grandparents cuz 3 generations are bad.

Kids may be sexualized but us elder Christians are not, so kindly clean your speech of this perverse rot!

SEPARATE MEANS HOLY

College administrators are the problem, caving into this and also radical faculty which are absurdly leftist.

The only way to adapt to the crazies was to go into total isolation or become part of them.

Guilt religion coming from Marxism (racism, race-baiting) is bringing down the west which is the best.

Denounce liberal terrorism before it's too late.

PC culture is an ideology rooted in constant new oppressions and finding new enemies to maintain power/aggressions

"A new social science paradigm and theoretician on par with Jung/Freud but with artistic significance."

LOW FAT AND LUSTROUS SKIN?

Answer to vegan stomach aches: Fruit/yogurt smoothies breakfast and miso/bean soup for lunch.

I feel so much better on the Old Lady Diet of fruit/yogurt smoothies and meso/bean soups/no more.

Fruits and soups are my way of escaping acid reflux, bloating, burping, insomnia and choking.

Lost 5 pounds on lowfat and dry skin problem is disappearing--enigma explained, its detoxing.

I'll persevere on the high fruit, high sugar/starch low fat diet. I'll never know what happens til I've tried it.

The skin is lustrous and so much better the lower the fat. It's been a month without any/love it like that.

Fat doesn't moisten the skin it just builds the false body of weird tissue, bulges, tags, jowls, this and that.

SEPARATE MEANS HOLY

Bean soups cooking for ten hours with aromas of herbs and heaven filling the house, every day it's like this.

Every time we eat trans fat we create more false body [ugly tissue] tho' many youth working out can get away with it.

LIGHTER, PURER, WISER

I'm the same way, extremely elastic. That's why I gotta restrain/moderate all I do or look sick.

If you ate too much yesterday, fast today. Don't let it build up, you'll be happier living this way.

Lighter, purer, wiser--you'll be even cleaner than before the fat cycle began. Ir's a miracle man.

God said wash all your red cashmere. I did and I feel enveloped in luxury and holiday cheer.

The world is so insane you must make your environment reflect your personality, then enhanced.

Listen: he awakened something in you but it's not him, it's who comes after him my friend.

This isn't the fifties in a sense of community it's becoming hellish in divisions you see.

Fortunately you get to the point where the past isn't so painful it's just bloody unbelievable.

No matter what you do they put an evil spin on it. If you love dogs & cats they'll call it bestiality.

Due to what they've already accepted liberals have dirty minds so get ready to be misdefined.

LIKE PSALMS SAYS THEY HATED YOU

SEPARATE MEANS HOLY

Like the Psalms says, they hated you for your dis-ease. Your sin, obstruction, missing the mark.

I think it was taken care of by a buncha underhanded women and that you caved into them.

Liberals: I can't stand them, been scared of em since Kindergarten. School phobia they call it.

It's a loud social atmosphere where chatter and hugging has precedence over substance.

I hated all that nonessential superfluity since a child and I still do, preferring the smallest room.

I find them despicable in their callous negligence all the while chattering to their fans/audience.

You think something's gonna take a month and God solves it in a moment, what a thought!

THE OTHERS ARE CALLOUS

The saints have such a stinging conscience they hurt while the others are seared: CALLOUS.

The preposterous untruth that morbid obesity can be considered healthy is the current falsity.

Stop cringing as you look back. Instead, self-congratulate you now know who to sack.

No matter how you see it, it's still self-gloating and red carpet mimicry when you're really lousy.

It's not true genius but self-gloating and social hypnotism trying to get mass approval.

That's not what this is about! Just do your work in silent devotion expecting nothing and grow up.

SEPARATE MEANS HOLY

God put talents in you but you're into something else: social acceptance without true diligence.

Dumbed down & wouldn't leave me alone, just like the kids hating Beethoven in a small town.

Just like it was with Einstein they'd travel far and wide just to debate me, until I set boundaries.

What difference would it make to them what I thought? Yet they were compelled to ARGUE/talk.

Ultimately it's how our Maker sees us after death. Not how we look like the Pharisees God saith.

If I see you're into THEIR reactions to you I lose interest so fast cuz It's about the work dude.

Your trip incites status-tension/aggression in anyone who sees you don't take it seriously.

Back then I caved into the liberal tyrants not knowing waz happening but now we'll see friend.

ALL FLUFF OR PERFORMANCE?

You are all fluff and no performance and I'm sick of it. Get your eyes offa them, get off of it.

Liberals destroy you when they can't debate you. They even commit crimes and justify em too.

Just get into your God-ordained work not shaking hands and smiling. That's fake success honey.

Take your eyes off others cuz it's just illusion they're getting ahead, they're the walking dead.

Due to bad habits he's aging before our eyes but at least he's making some money before he dies.

P.S. God solves problems in the most clever ways-- unimaginable things you'd never think or say.

100 KAREN KELLOCK BOOKS

AFFINITY OR MISERY
AGELESS CORNUCOPIA
AMERICA AWAKE!
AMERICA'S DAFT ERA
ARTS OF PALEO FASTING
AUTOPHAGY ON CHEATERS
BACKSTABBING NEUROTICS
BETRAYAL TRAUMA
BOOMERS AND BROKENNESS
BOOT ON NECK
CHAMPION GUIDES
COMMIE NUTHOUSE
COMMIES
COMMUNIST SPIRIT
CONTAGION OF MADNESS
CONTAGIOUS MADNESS
CULTURE CLASH BASHED
DAFT LEFT
DAILY FASTARIAN
DAM RATS
DIVERSITY IS CRUELTY
E-RACE WHITE
EVIL FREAKS (Beyond Gross)
THE END OR A BEND?
FEMALE BULLIES AND FEMI-NAZIS
FEMALE CARNALITY
FEMALE DUMB DOWN
FEMALE POWER DRIVE
FEMINISM AND RUIN 1 & 2
FIX FOR MISFITS
FOOLS & TRAMPS
FREEDOM SPEAKING
FRENEMY ENABLER
FRENEMY LIAR
FRENEMY THIEF
FRENEMY TRAITOR
TRENEMY TYRANT
GENIUS IS HELD DOWN
GLOBALISLAM
GOD USES THE FLAWED
HAZE OF THE LATTER DAYS

THE HERD IN WORDS
HIX POLITIX
HOW THEY RUINED US
JUST SKIP DINNER
LE FEMME AND THE COMMUNIST SPIRIT
LIBERAL CHAOS & ROT
LIBERAL DOUBLETHINK
LIBERAL GALL 1 & 2
LIBERAL SHOVE-DOWNS
LOCK YOUR GATE
LOSERS and Femme Fatales
MANUAL FOR SUPERIOR MEN
MODERN ART FROM HELL
MOSTLY FAKE
NOTES TO CHAMPS 1 & 2
OVERCOME FRENEMIES
PC MAKES US CRAZY
PEOPLE ARE CRUEL
PEOPLE PROBLEMS 1 & 2
PERSECUTED GENIUIS
POLI-PSYCH MYSTERIES
PRETENTIOUS SLOBS
QUEEN BEE
RED NEW DEAL
RETURNING TO FIRST NATURE
SEASON OF TREASON
SEPARATE MEANS HOLY
SOCIAL HYPNOTISM
SOLITUDE SOLUTION
SUPERCILIOUS
THE SCHOOLS SCREWED EM UP
TOAD TO PRINCE
TRIALS CYCLES
TRUMP VS. GROUP
TRUST IN TRASH
THE TRUTH ABOUT PEOPLE
UNDERHEANDEDLY CLEVER
WALK TALL WITHIN WALLS
WE'RE NOT ALL ONE
WINNERS SKIP DINNER
WORK OR SMERK

KAREN KELLOCK PH.D.

M.S. Political Science, San Diego State. Ph.D. in Psychology, University of California Irvine. Postdoctoral: UCI School of Medicine, Dept. of Psychiatry [NIMH Grants]. Developed the Debris Theory of Disease, a theory of system pathology in 120 books and 22 textbooks for the general public. The theory has a general formula: All disease is obstruction, all recovery is elimination, all success is attraction. The three obstructions are people, habit and food. Remove obstruction and snap to your goals, waiting in the wings.

www.ingramcontent.com/pod-product-compliance
Lightning Source LLC
Chambersburg PA
CBHW061721250726

48657CB00002B/717